C4

95

CW00422526

THE GUARDIAN BOOK OF
THE GENERAL STRIKE

The Guardian Book of the General Strike

R.H. HAIGH
D.S. MORRIS
A.R. PETERS

WILDWOOD HOUSE

Published by
Wildwood House Limited
Gower House
Croft Road
Aldershot
Hants GU11 3HR
England

Distributed in the United States by
Gower Publishing Company
Old Post Road
Brookfield
Vermont 05036
USA

The reports in this book, all from the pages of the *Manchester
Guardian*, were selected by three independent historians who
also wrote the annotations, introduction and appendices.

British Library Cataloguing in Publication Data
The Guardian book of the General Strike.
   1. General Strike, Great Britain, 1926 ————
Sources
I. Haigh, R H   II. Morris, D S   III. Peters, A R
(Anthony R)   IV. Manchester Guardian
331.89′25′0941   HD5365.A6

ISBN 0-7045-3081-3

Printed and bound in Great Britain by
Billing and Sons Limited, Worcester.

Contents

Acknowledgements

A number of people have made our task in producing this book a great deal easier than would have otherwise been the case. Michael Harkin, Social Sciences Librarian at the Central Library in Manchester, responded most readily to our request for microfilmed copies of the *Manchester Guardian* and, by so doing, greatly reduced the time and effort expended on producing the manuscript. The staff of the Eric Mensforth Library, Sheffield City Polytechnic, all gave willingly of their time and never failed to meet the many arduous demands we made of them. Ruth Barker cheerfully undertook the typing entailed in preparing the manuscript for publication with the utmost speed and accuracy.

Finally we dedicate this book to our families.

R.H. Haigh
D.S. Morris
A.R. Peters
Sheffield, 1987

Editors' Introduction to the Series

The historian is blessed with many advantages. He can assemble all of the available facts relevant to any particular past event, analyse each in turn, assemble his accumulated knowledge into a comprehensive and logically sequential pattern, and present a rationally sound appraisal of all the elements which have contributed both directly and indirectly to a social phenomenon considered by him or by others to be worthy of special attention.

In marked contrast to the historian stands the journalist. Not for him the luxury of wide-ranging and detailed information; instead he is confronted by a complex blend of fact, rumour and innuendo which falls far short of being comprehensive in character or cohesive in format. Working from partial information he can at best offer his reader a rational assessment of what he has gleaned from a multiplicity of sources, with but little hope or opportunity of being able to verify and validate every element of his story by reference to other knowledgeable or accepted authorities and accounts.

Yet despite the advantages enjoyed by the historian and despite the disadvantages which beset the journalist, there is an immediacy about journalistic accounts which the historian can only try to capture in his own scholarly labours. Social events rarely happen in a causal sequence, decisions are invariably taken on the basis of limited knowledge, and the complexity of societal phenomena makes total comprehension and a fully rational response an impossibility. Perhaps, therefore, the historian may be not unreasonably accused of enforcing a rationality and order on to events which is largely his own, and of attributing motives which accord with his perceptions rather than being the motives which underlay human actions at the time of his chosen event.

In short the journalist offers a 'snap shot' of the world as he perceives it in the present, an assessment which has an immediacy even though it affords an interpretation which may well lack comprehensiveness. The historian working from accumulated past knowledge and enjoying the benefit of hindsight, is able to offer a fuller account of past events but one which will almost inevitably fall short of conveying the immediacy which is a feature of the journalistic report.

Let it not be forgotten that the work of a journalist can, of itself, be a factor which influences the actions of others. Journalistic accounts are themselves elements which are capable of influencing the perceptions and behaviours of social actors and can, therefore, be an integral part of significant events in man's social activities. The historian may point to past 'errors' and may influence current and future events by so doing, but it is most unlikely that his work will ever, by its very nature, be as significant a determinant of current events as that of the journalist.

This is not to deny or denigrate the art of the historian. It is simply to state that in order to gain an understanding of a past event and to acquire an appreciation of it that was available to the majority of those living at the time it was unfolding, it may well be more fruitful to give consideration to journalistic accounts of the day rather than simply being restricted to the more academically oriented accounts of historians. Journalists offer living history, historians offer considered history. Neither is, of itself, better than the other, nor are the two mutually exclusive. We have chosen to portray the General Strike of May 1926 through the pages of the *Manchester Guardian* and, by so doing, have consciously sought to offer a counterbalance to the many voluminous and more profoundly academic accounts which have been produced over the years.

Whether or not we have succeeded must be left to the judgement of the reader.

R.H. Haigh
D.S. Morris
A.R. Peters
Sheffield, 1987

Chronology of Events

1888	Formation of the Miners Federation of Great Britain.
1906	Trades Dispute Act protects union funds from legal action while in furtherance of an industrial dispute.
	Twenty-nine Labour Party members elected to Parliament.
1911	Mines Act improves safety standards.
1912	Minimum Wage Act.
1913	Trade Union Act legalises the 'political levy'.
1914	Triple Alliance of transport workers, miners and railway workers formed.
1916	Wartime government takes effective control of mines.
1917	Bolshevik revolution ousts provisional government in Russia.
1919	Railway strike leads to establishment of measures supervised by the Supply and Transport Committee of the Cabinet to maintain essential services.
	Government establishes the Sankey Commission to defuse strike threat by miners. Interim Report recommendation of nationalisation not accepted by government.
1920	Dockers refuse to load ship sending supplies to oppose Red Army intervention in Poland. TUC and Labour Party state opposition to British military intervention in Poland.
	Communist Party formed in Britain.
1921	Government states intention to return mines to private ownership. In response to owners' demands for wage cuts, MFGB calls on Triple Alliance to halt movement of coal. Strike collapses

1921	April 15 – Black Friday. Herbert Smith becomes President of MFGB.
1924	January–November, first Labour government led by Ramsay MacDonald. The Conservative Party under Stanley Baldwin wins election held on October 29 amid rumours of linkages between Moscow and the British Communist Party seeking to promote revolution (Zinoviev letter). A.J. Cook becomes Secretary of MFGB. Labour Party moves to purge Communists within its ranks.
1925	Britain returns to the Gold Standard in April, reducing international competitiveness of British coal and leading to further demands for wage cuts. MFGB calls on TUC to support coal embargo. Baldwin capitulates on July 30 (Red Friday) and agrees to nine-month subsidy pending report of a Royal Commission. In August Tory backbenchers demand pledge not to renew subsidy after April 1926. In September government appoints Samuel Commission and alongside formation of OMS sets in motion covert preparations to counter a General Strike. Twelve Communist Party members arrested and imprisoned on charges of seditious libel and incitement to mutiny in October. In November Ministry of Health Circular 636 notifying local authorities of preparations to maintain essential services in the event of a general strike is prepared. TUC agrees in December to maintain Industrial Committee used as negotiating body in July dispute but confirms that the decision to strike remains a matter for individual unions not the TUC.
1926	
January	First of a series of conferences organised by the government held over three months at local and national level to co-ordinate preparations to maintain transport and police services in the event of a General Strike. Walter Citrine, General Secretary of the TUC, urges the General Council to prepare for strike action. His recommendations are largely ignored by the TUC.
March 6	Samuel Commission completes its Report, which is published on the 11th.

March 25–31	Report discussed in meetings between Mining Association and MFGB. Government promises legislation if both parties can agree on a settlement.
April 13	Complete deadlock in negotiations.
14	Industrial Committee of the General Council of the TUC calls on Baldwin to intervene.
15	Baldwin discusses the position with MFGB.
21	Baldwin discusses the situation with Mining Association.
22	MFGB and Mining Association meet again but still deadlocked over owners' demands for district wage agreements and lowering of minimum wage.
23	MFGB announces delegate conference to be held on 28th. TUC summons conference of union executives on 29th with suggestion that it would be used to endorse strike action.
27	TUC General Council sets up Ways and Means Committee to organise strike preparations. Industrial Committee repeats its conviction that the solution lies in government support for the Samuel Report in full.
28	At the MFGB delegates conference Cook repeats determination to resist wage cuts.
29	Conference of Union Executives urges Baldwin to press Mining Association to drop its demand for district agreements.
30	Mining Association offers national agreement but on the basis of a reduction in the minimum wage and longer hours. Proposals rejected by MFGB and with the lockout due to commence at midnight, government prepares to declare a State of Emergency and despatch Circular 699 to activate framework to maintain services. Last-ditch efforts by Industrial Committee to reach agreement with Baldwin balked by miners' insistence on clarification of reorganisation proposals before acceptance of wage cuts.
May 1	Conference of trade union executives votes overwhelmingly to support strike action from midnight May 3 and hand over conduct or the dispute to the General Council of the TUC. TUC

May 1	later denies that it agreed not to enter into a negotiated settlement of the dispute without the prior approval of the MFGB.
	General Council offer to collaborate with government in maintenance of transport and food supplies snubbed.
	Indications of a truce established when Baldwin and the Industrial Committee agree on a formula for further negotiations.
2	Truce formula collapses when Cook insists that it be put to the full executive of the MFGB, already dispersed to all parts of the country to organise the strike. Industrial Committee forced to await recall of executive and finally returns to Downing Street at 9 p.m. instead of 1 p.m. as previously agreed. Cabinet, infuriated by delay and the report of *Daily Mail* incident, elects to break off negotiations and demand unconditional abandonment of strike.
3	Further attempts at negotiation blocked by government insistence on unconditional surrender.
4	Three and a half million workers on strike in response to TUC call for stoppage in specified 'first line' industries. Strike run centrally by Ernest Bevin's Strike Organisation Committee and locally co-ordinated by the Trades Councils. OMS merges with government network and volunteers begin skeleton services to maintain transport and unload ships. Naval ratings used to assist in keeping power stations in operation.
5	First issues of the *British Gazette* and the *British Worker* appear as propaganda mouthpieces for the two sides. Under Churchill's editorship the *Gazette* labels the strike as a challenge to the constitutional order. Violent outbursts in several cities occur as strikers clash with volunteers and the police.
6	Sir John Simon in the House of Commons contends that the 1906 Trades Dispute Act does not cover the present dispute and therefore union funds are not immune from compensation demanded for breach of contract.
	Sir Herbert Samuel returns to Britain.
7	Samuel begins discussions with TUC.
	Archbishop of Canterbury refused permission to broadcast settlement appeal on the BBC.

8	Twenty armoured cars and detachments of two Guards regiments escort food convoy from London docks to Hyde Park. Government calls for enlistment in Civil Constabulary Reserve and *British Gazette* urges Armed Forces to take all 'necessary steps' to maintain order.
9	Flying squadrons of soldiers and special police moved into the centre of London amid speculation that the government intends to arrest the trade union leadership.
10	Discussions between Sir Herbert Samuel and the Industrial Committee result in an agreement based upon continuation of the subsidy and reference of the dispute to a National Wages Board. Miners reject the Samuel Memorandum and insist that the strike continue until assurances are received from the government that the Samuel recommendations will be implemented in full. Cabinet discusses proposal to prevent banks paying strike benefits.
11	Mr Justice Astbury in the High Court confirms the illegality of the strike and grants an injunction to prevent union officers calling out on strike a branch of the National Sailors' and Firemen's Union. Cabinet discusses a bill to define illegal strikes and ban the use of union funds to support illegal strikes. King George V, unknown to the public, warns Cabinet against taking further action to limit the ability of the unions to provide strike pay.
12	TUC General Council fails to persuade miners to accept Samuel Memorandum but goes ahead with plan to present proposals to the Prime Minister. At 12.20 p.m. the deputation from the General Council informs Baldwin that the strike will be called off and urges the government to adopt the Samuel Memorandum as a basis for a settlement. Baldwin agrees to consider the Memorandum but gives no assurance that it will be accepted. BBC broadcasts news that the strike is over but miners inform regions that they should not return to work until the situation is reviewed by a delegates' conference on May 14.
13	While the *British Gazette* crows over 'unconditional surrender' the *British Worker* claims that the General Council has been able to negotiate a satisfactory settlement with the government. Local

May 13	strike committees facing the continuation of the lockout and threats of victimisation against strike leaders in many areas elect to continue the strike. In response to Ramsay MacDonald's plea in the House of Commons, Baldwin issues a statement that the government 'will not countenance' victimisation of strikers by owners.
14–31	Individual unions negotiate terms for a return to work but many men and women are not reinstated or suffer a humiliating revision of their conditions of service. Baldwin outlines the basis for a settlement of the mining dispute but it is rejected by both parties. As a result the miners continue their strike and the government withdraws its offer to continue the subsidy while its terms are implemented.
June	Emergency Powers still retained and while the government introduces legislation to promote the amalgamation of smaller collieries and impose a levy on mining royalties, the suspension of the seven-hour working day represents another blow to the miners.
September	Mining Association rejects repeated government calls for negotiations to be resumed on the basis of a search for a national settlement.
November–December	Strike ends with the miners' capitulation to the owners' demands for district agreements, a lower subsistence wage and longer hours.
1927	
May	Conservative government introduces Trades Dispute and Trade Union Act that outlaws the general strike and reduces the political muscle of the unions by limiting the ability of the unions to extract a 'political levy' from their workforce.

A Guide to the Main Characters

Astbury, Mr Justice: Rose to prominence during the strike for his ruling in the Chancery Division of the High Court that officials of the Seamen's Union were not empowered to call out their members on strike in support of the miners. This decision basically confirmed Simon's declaration that the General Strike was illegal and suggested that the unions were open to legal action as a result of being in breach of contract.

Baldwin, Stanley: Prime Minister. A former Chancellor of the Exchequer, Baldwin had led a coup against the inner circle of the Tory Party in 1922 that resulted in the unseating of Lloyd George as coalition leader and his own elevation into the limelight. Although uncertain as to his standing with the party hierarchy, Baldwin presented the image of a man of conciliation and national unity that was popular with the public and the postwar wave of young Tory backbenchers.

Bevin, Ernest: General Secretary of the TGWU and leading figure in the national co-ordination and running of the strike. From a poor background and a basic elementary education Bevin had worked his way up through the dockers' union and was the architect of the TGWU formed in 1921. A respected figure within the union movement who clearly held misgivings as to the wisdom of the General Strike, Bevin was a key figure in the attempts to negotiate a solution through the creation of a National Wages Board.

Birkenhead, Lord: Oxford-educated barrister who had been a member of the aristocratic inner circle of the Tory Party for over a decade. Secretary for India at the time of the strike but a leading figure in the negotiations with the TUC. His initial sympathy for the miners was generated by his annoyance at the obstinacy displayed by the Mining Association. After May 3, however, he swung behind the Cabinet line, seeing the strike as a challenge to the constitution which therefore necessitated the demand for unconditional surrender.

Churchill, Winston: Grandson of the Duke of Marlborough and educated at Harrow. He originally joined the Liberal Party after a colourful episode as a soldier and war correspondent but moved to the Tory Party in 1924. Chancellor of the Exchequer at the time of the strike and editor of the *British Gazette*, Churchill led the 'hawks' in the Cabinet linking the strike with the menace of international communism.

Citrine, Walter: General Secretary of the TUC who had urged the General Council in January 1926 to begin systematic preparations for a general strike. Citrine, however, was no left-wing firebrand. In essence he was representative of the new breed of union bureaucrats who saw the need to establish a strong and efficient central administrative machine to improve the bargaining power of the labour movement.

Clynes, J.R.: Official of the National Union of General and Municipal Workers and a Labour MP post 1906 serving as Lord Privy Seal in MacDonald's first government. As a former leader of the party Clynes was a central figure alongside MacDonald in urging the miners to be flexible in pursuit of a settlement.

Cook, A.J.: Secretary of the Miners Federation, born in Somerset but raised in the South Wales coalfield. Associated with the prewar syndicalist movement. A public speaker with an evangelical approach, fond of painting a stark class-based analysis of British society.

Davidson, J.C.C.: Tory MP and Private Secretary to Baldwin. During the strike he held the influential office of Deputy Civil Service Commissioner in charge of Press and Radio. Although he resisted Churchill's desire to use the media to discredit and violently attack the unions, Davidson played a central role in ensuring that John Reith at the BBC understood the picture of the situation that the government wished the BBC to reinforce.

Joynson-Hicks, Sir William: Home Secretary closely associated with the 'hawks' in the Cabinet. Clearly saw the strike as communist-inspired and a threat to the basic pillars of British society.

Lloyd George, David: Charismatic Liberal MP who held the position of Prime Minister from 1916 to 1922. From the outset he rejected the suggestion that the strike was a threat to the constitutional order and led parliamentary condemnation of the inflammatory statements issued by the *British Gazette*. His speech on May 10 ridiculing the decision by the BBC to deny the Archbishop of Canterbury the opportunity to broadcast an appeal for a settlement of the dispute was a significant factor in the subsequent reversal of the decision.

Macdonald, James Ramsey: The first Labour Prime Minister in 1924. MacDonald was a legend within the socialist movement. From joining the Fabian Society in 1886 MacDonald had played a central part in the birth and construction of the Labour Party. Despite his penchant for fiery rhetoric he was closely allied with the moderates within the movement who favoured gradualism and the acceptance of the need to work through the existing parliamentary process in order to achieve power. As a result, while outwardly supporting the miners' cause he was a central figure in the attempts to persuade the unions to negotiate an early settlement. It would appear that his concern was generated largely by the fear that the strike would be used by the Tories to discredit the Labour Party as a responsible force in British politics.

Pugh, Arthur: General Secretary of the Iron and Steel Trades Confederation. Succeeded A.B. Swales as Chairman of the TUC General Council in 1925 and was representative of the swing in the TUC leadership in this period towards moderation. Pugh was described by the *Daily Herald* as 'a capable man of business' who 'could have made a fortune as a chartered accountant'.

Saklatvala, Sharpurti: Communist MP for Battersea North arrested on May 4 for urging the armed forces to lay down their weapons. Charged with sedition, he was sentenced to two months' imprisonment.

Samuel, Sir Herbert: Oxford-educated Liberal politician who held a succession of Cabinet posts in the Liberal administrations from 1909 to 1916, culminating in the office of Home Secretary in 1916. High Commissioner for Palestine 1920–25. Returned to Britain in 1925 to chair the Royal Commission on the Coal Industry. Samuel played a central role during the strike in negotiations with the TUC to find the basis for a settlement. At no time, however, was this role agreed with the government and there was no commitment from Baldwin to support the Samuel Memorandum.

Simon, Sir John: Oxford-educated barrister who was elected as a Liberal MP in 1906 and served as Home Secretary 1915–16. Widely respected for his legal acumen, his speech delivered to the House of Commons on May 6 1926 was arguably a key consideration in persuading the TUC to seek a settlement. Simon argued that the strike was illegal in that a dispute did not exist between the government and the TUC. In consequence the strikers were in breach of contract and liable to be pursued for damages by their employers. Although widely accepted at the time, Simon's opinion was subsequently rejected by a string of eminent lawyers.

Smith, Herbert: Born in the workhouse in Kippax, Leeds, in 1862; first entered the mines at the age of 10. A dour negotiator known for the phrase 'nowt doing', Smith became President of the Yorkshire Miners in 1905 and President of the MFGB in 1922.

Steel-Maitland, Sir Arthur: Oxford-educated Tory MP, Minister for Labour 1924–29. Played a central role in the negotiations of March and April 1926 and was seen as one of the moderates within the Cabinet anxious to avoid a confrontation. Used as an intermediary by Baldwin during the strike to warn Samuel that his negotiations with the TUC were entirely unofficial.

Thomas, James Henry: A former engine driver on the GWR who worked his way up through the ranks of the NUR to the post of General Secretary in 1917. Also a Labour MP and Colonial Secretary in MacDonald's first government. Seen as an able and accomplished negotiator but mistrusted by the left wing of the labour movement because of his willingness to deal with the 'establishment'. Throughout the strike Thomas was one of the leading union figures seeking compromise and the abandonment of what he saw as a dangerous confrontation that threatened the future credibility of the labour movement.

The Background to the Dispute

Now the country faces the terrible blasting devastating menace of a general strike... ...a general strike will inevitably lead to some Soviet of Trade Unions with real control of the country and the effectual subversion of the state. (Winston Churchill, Chancellor of Exchequer on the eve of the General Strike.)

The object of a lockout is to deprive people of food until they agree to dictated terms. . . . Those who foolishly call the 1926 affair 'a challenge to Democracy' should remember that it began by an attempt to starve a million workmen and their families. (J.R. Clynes, a former leader of the Labour Party. Quotation taken from J.R. Clynes, *Memoirs Vol 2*, (London, 1937) p.76.

These quotations are indicative of the controversy and debate that have surrounded the events of May 1926. For some observers the General Strike was simply a sympathetic action launched by the trade union movement in support of the miners' campaign for a seven-hour working day and 'a living wage'. An alternative view has been proposed by commentators who claim to have identified, behind the facade of a dispute over pay and conditions of work, the hand of the radical left seeking to promote revolution and overthrow the central pillars of British society. These perspectives are not necessarily irreconcilable; there may be an element of truth in both. Certainly the coalmining industry employing approximately one and a quarter million men in 1926, had been badly hit by the postwar economic slump. In a situation where the decline in the demand for coal was squeezing, and at times almost eliminating, profit levels, the colliery owners' demands for austerity and a reduction in wage levels were contemptuously resisted by the miners. If, therefore, in 1926 open warfare was to be declared in the field of industrial relations, it was probable that the mining industry, with its history of thinly veiled hostility between the workforce and the mine owners, would be the battlefield upon which the first clashes would occur.

Yet the Miners Federation of Great Britain could hardly be seen as an agent for radical change in British society. Although sections of the union had flirted in the prewar period with the syndicalist movement seeking to promote worker control of industry and had joined in 1914 with the railwaymen and the transport workers to form a Triple Alliance to bolster their collective bargaining power, in general the MFGB, since its creation in 1893, had limited its demands to acceptance of the need for national standards outlining wage levels, hours of work and safety conditions. This campaign, however, was actively opposed by the majority of the colliery owners, who saw the miners' claims as being inflated and unrealistic. It was argued that, given that mine ownership was divided between over a thousand individual companies operating under markedly different circumstances, wage bargaining could only be conducted at a local level and had to reflect varying levels of profitability. The imposition of a minimum wage would build in overheads that would prevent the industry from responding to fluctuations in domestic and international markets and erode the industry's competitive edge. In emphasising the need to respond to market forces the coal owners rejected the charges levelled by the miners that low levels of profitability were a result of under investment and poor management and refuted the suggestion that nationalisation of the industry was in the best interests of both the workforce and the nation.

Between the two sides stood the government. Although in the immediate prewar era Asquith's Liberal government appeared sympathetic to the miners' cause, introducing legislation accepting the principle of a minimum wage and measures to improve safety standards in the collieries, there was certainly no indication of support for the eventual nationalisation of the industry. In reality, it was accepted that the government had a responsibility to assist those living at or below subsistence level, but state intervention was designed to strengthen rather than replace the market mechanism.

The problems of the coal industry came to a head in the postwar era when British domination of domestic and foreign markets was threatened by competition from European producers and the emerging industrial might of the United States. In addition, the primacy of coal as the source of industrial fuel was challenged by oil. In an increasingly volatile market it was evident that, although wartime demand had led to an expansion in productive capacity, there had been a general reluctance to engage in investment and replace what was often already antiquated equipment. As a consequence efficiency had fallen and British coal was threatened by cheaper foreign competition. To an extent this situation was initially obscured by the postwar industrial boom which inflated the demand for coal and deterred competitive price cutting on the international market. In the domestic arena further stability was provided by the continuation of the controls imposed by the government in the latter years of the war over price, wage and profit levels.

These props, however, were removed when, after 1920, a sudden decline in industrial demand saw coal prices spiral rapidly downwards. In anticipation of such a collapse and the inevitable demand for wage reductions that would result from the colliery owners, the miners in 1919 had returned to their campaign for the nationalisation of the industry. To an extent the government appeared prepared to respond to their demands and, in exchange for the withdrawal of a threat to undertake strike action, the Prime Minister, Lloyd George, agreed to appoint a Royal Commission to examine the state of the industry. The resulting recommendations, known as the Sankey Report, largely supported the miners' case by advocating the complete reorganisation of the industry, incorporating major improvements in wages and conditions of service and, most significantly, the Commission supported the case for nationalisation of the industry. The jubilation of the MFGB was, however, shortlived for, while accepting the principle of action to improve wage levels and formalise a seven-hour working day, the government rejected nationalisation in favour of an examination of a proposal to nationalise the royalties received by owners of the land on which the collieries were situated and encouragement of a wider role for the workforce in running the industry. To add insult to injury it was announced that the mines would be returned to private ownership on March 31 1921. On reciept of this news the owners immediately declared their intention to lock out the workforce on that date if agreement was not reached on the principle of district rather than national bargaining and acceptance of immediate wage cuts or a lengthening of the working day.

The two sides appeared set on a collision course when the miners rejected the owners' terms and called on the Triple Alliance to halt the production and movement of coal throughout the country in defence of the miners' existing terms of service. The situation, however, was defused when the strike call, scheduled for April 15 1921, was abandoned following disagreement within the ranks of the MFGB as to the advisability of entering into negotiations for district agreements. It was evident that the Triple Alliance was far from firm in its resolve to pursue strike action and the other unions, in the face of Lloyd George's threat to declare a state of emergency and use the armed forces to maintain essential services, were only too ready to use the division within the ranks of the MFGB as a pretext to abandon the strike.

The whole affair was a tragedy for the miners, who were locked out for three months before surrendering to the owners' terms. The trade union movement drew several significant lessons from the events surrounding April 15 1921, which was later known simply as 'Black Friday'. Firstly, it was clear that it had been a mistake to suspend strike action in 1919 without a prior commitment from the government not only to establish but also to act upon the recommendations of the Royal Commission. Secondly, it was evident that a body was needed to coordinate collaboration between unions when undertaking industrial action. It was decided that in future the General Council of the TUC would be a suitable agent to undertake this role, although there was no suggestion that the unions would automatically surrender their autonomy to this central body.

Alongside this review of tactics and structures, significant changes were being undertaken within the MFGB in this period with the installation of Herbert Smith as President of the Union. Smith, a former prize fighter who revelled in the image of being a dour Yorkshireman, soon became known as a firm and uncompromising negotiator. A.J. Cook, who was appointed General Secretary to the Union in 1924, was on the other hand a far more volatile character. Closely associated with the prewar syndicalist movement in the coalfields of South Wales, Cook was renowned throughout the MFGB for his fiery speeches that painted a stark class-based analysis of British society and condemned the greed and corruption of the owners. Although in many ways as different as chalk and cheese, together Smith and Cook were a formidable team who would clearly resist any further assaults on the miners' standard of living.

The first serious test of their commitment came in 1925, when the mineowners demanded the acceptance of further wage cuts. To an extent the situation was precipitated by competition from the German coalfields, but the position was also severely exacerbated by the government's decision to return to the Gold Standard. This move effectively overvalued sterling and eroded the coal industry's remaining competitive edge in international markets. From the outset the miners declared their determination to resist the owners' terms, pointing to managerial inefficiency and the hidden profits contained in transfer pricing as major contributory factors to the industry's problems. It seemed that a confrontation was inevitable when the owners announced that a lockout would commence on July 31 1925 unless their terms were accepted.

As an indication of their determination to avoid the mistakes of 1921 the MFGB refused to collaborate with a Court of Inquiry established by the government and sought the support of the General Council of the TUC for an embargo by the transport unions on the movement of coal. Faced with an apparent determination to paralyse the distribution of the nation's primary source of energy, the Prime Minister, Stanley Baldwin, capitulated. On what was subsequently termed 'Red Friday', Baldwin agreed to maintain wage levels through the provision of a government subsidy until May 1926 pending the examination of the state of the coal industry by a further Royal Commission.

Although it was widely conceded within the General Council of the TUC that 'Red Friday' was only a temporary truce in the dispute between the miners and colliery owners, the euphoria surrounding the events of July 1925 appeared to dull rather than sharpen the appreciation in the trade union movement of the need to prepare for a possible further clash when the subsidy ended on April 30 1926. While it was agreed to retain the Special Industrial Committee of the TUC, which had been the main negotiating body for the unions in July 1925, the only positive move to strengthen union solidarity in the following six months was a tentative and largely inconclusive attempt to establish an alliance of unions representing the miners, railwaymen, electricians and foundrymen.

The stance adopted by the unions in this period could perhaps be seen as complacent following the success of Red Friday and certainly seemed to show an implicit faith in the ability of the Royal Commission to identify the grounds for a satisfactory settlement. It would appear, however, that the government did not share this optimism and was, from the outset, anticipating the likelihood of a further industrial clash. In the event of such a confrontation it was evident that large sections of the Conservative Party, while appreciating that the lack of adequate preparations necessitated a tactical retreat in July 1925, had no intention of allowing the unions to pressurise the government into further concessions. For many Tory diehards the shadow of the Bolshevik revolution and the growth of the British Communist movement were seen as a cancer to be confronted and eliminated before the communists could gain control of the trade union movement.

In the latter half of 1925 the government set in motion preparations to maintain transport, food supplies and security during a state of emergency. Although the most visible manifestation of activity was the creation of an ostensibly independent body, the Organisation for the Maintenance of Supplies (OMS), to establish a register of volunteers prepared to man essential services, the real groundwork was undertaken behind the scenes by the Supply and Transport Committee of the Cabinet. By the early months of 1926 detailed preparations had been made for the division of the country into a number of regions, each headed by a Civil Commissioner. In the event of a transport strike a State of Emergency would be declared and the Commissioners would assume responsibility for the maintenance of food, transport and fuel supplies in collaboration with local government and industry. While it was anticipated that co-operation would be voluntary, the Commissioners held extensive powers to commandeer premises and equipment and maintain order through the enlistment of special constables. It was made clear that in exceptional circumstances the armed forces would be available to man essential services and maintain order.

If the trade unions were slow to appreciate the extent and the nature of the preparations being undertaken by the government, there were in this period more overt indications of a determination to counter what was seen as the growing influence of the radical left in British politics. In October 1925 twelve members of the Communist Party were arrested and imprisoned for up to twelve months for seditious libel and incitement to mutiny. The ransacking of the Communist Party offices and the removal of senior party figures from active involvement in party and union affairs suggested that the government was anticipating a large-scale industrial struggle in 1926 and was determined to reduce the power base of the Communist Party.

While this move was not entirely unwelcome amongst the ranks of the trade unions and the Labour Party, it was accompanied by a more subtle strike against the left, the decision not to repeat the exercise of 1921 of inviting the MFGB to nominate members to serve on the Royal Commission. It was announced that the Commission would be headed by Sir Herbert Samuel, a former Liberal Home Secretary. He was to be assisted by William Beveridge, Director of the LSE, General Sir Herbert Lawrence, Managing Director of the bankers Glyn, Mills and Co., and Kenneth Lee, Chairman of the cotton manufacturers Tootal. None of the members held prior knowledge of the coal industry and, while it was agreed that they were likely to display sympathy for the miners' cause, there was little indication of support for the concept of nationalisation.

The Royal Commission heard evidence on the problems and state of the mining industry from 76 witnesses over a period of four months before finally publishing its report on March 11 1926. In the long term the report repeated the call for the nationalisation of mining royalties and advocated the voluntary reorganisation of the industry with the amalgamation of smaller collieries and the improvement of working conditions and terms of service. In the short term, however, while existing hour levels were defended, the report saw no alternative to the discontinuation of the subsidy and a reduction in wage levels. It was emphasised, though, that wages should not fall below identified subsistence levels, that the principle of a national norm should be retained and that concessions on reductions should only be accepted alongside agreement on long term reform.

The response to the report was cautious from both sides. The miners sought clarification of the precise nature of long term reform, while the colliery owners focused specifically on the format and extent of the wage cuts. It soon became apparent, however, that the reluctance of the owners to commit themselves to a reorganisation of the industry would lead to deadlock on the more immediate problem of wage levels. On this basis the negotiations quickly ground to a standstill and the situation appeared ripe for a government initiative to bring the two sides together and break the impasse that had been reached. For almost a month, however, Baldwin played a curiously muted role. Outwardly the Prime Minister maintained that it was for the miners and colliery owners to resolve their differences without government interference. Although it could be contended that Baldwin deliberately allowed the confrontation to escalate in the belief that the two sides would finally turn to him in desperation and allow him to impose a settlement, it could also be argued that the Prime Minister either sadly misread the situation or was spoiling for a fight. With the declared intention of the mineowners to lock out the workforce at midnight on April 30 unless lower wages or a longer working week were accepted, a major confrontation appeared imminent.

Three days before the expiry of the deadline the TUC at last began to face up to the implications of a commitment to support the miners. While the decision to establish a Ways and Means Committee to co-ordinate trade union activity in the event of strike action was indicative of the broad support for the miners within the ranks of the trade union movement and the Labour Party, there were already signs of a division of opinion beneath the thin veneer of solidarity. As April 30 drew closer there were clear indications that senior figures within both the TUC and the Labour Party were urging the miners to abandon their dogmatic resistance to cuts in wages or an increase in hours and be seen to be prepared to consider any new initiatives that might be placed on the table. This concern was based, not simply on the need to gain popular sympathy, but also on the fear that a large scale strike would be portrayed by the government as a communist-inspired challenge to the constitutional order. In such a situation the Labour Party's ability to pursue a 'moderate' path would be challenged and a pretext would be established for future legislation to restrict trade union rights. In addition, there was also a fear within the senior ranks of the Labour movement that a strike, once initiated, might be manipulated by communists to discredit the union leadership and escalate into open warfare. In reality the leadership of the MFGB was by no means as inflexible as official statements suggested but, caught between the demands of the mineowners and the expectations of their rank and file membership, Smith and Cook saw little option but to continue to reject the suggestion that agreement could be reached on wages before the details of long term reconstruction were hammered out.

If by the end of April there were signs of doubt within the Labour movement as to the advisability of initiating a widespread strike and lack of clarity on what would constitute an 'acceptable' settlement, there were certainly similar divisions within the ranks of the government and the colliery owners. Yet the mineowners who favoured a more conciliatory approach were clearly in a minority and held little influence within the leadership of the Mining

Association. Similarly, while senior members of the Conservative Party privately denounced the inflexibility of the owners, the decision to set in motion plans for the declaration of a state of emergency on April 30 and activate the preparations undertaken to counter a strike clearly suggested that if a conflict occurred it would be seen as a challenge to the constitutional authority of the government and the Conservative Party would close ranks in its determination to extract unconditional surrender from the trade union movement.

The events of May 1926 are told here through the pages of the *Manchester Guardian*. Although crippled along with the rest of the national press by the decision of the TUC to call out the print unions as part of the first wave of the stoppage, the *Manchester Guardian* managed to produce a scaled-down version of the paper throughout the strike. Through its pages accounts are provided of the nine-day strike and the negotiations that led to the decision on May 12 to return to work.

SELECTED REPORTS FROM THE
MANCHESTER GUARDIAN

APRIL 30 TO MAY 21 1926

IN SUSPENSE

Negotiations behind the scenes have continued without interruption during the last few days, and nothing, so far as the public is aware, has come of them to encourage the hope that a stoppage in the mining industry will be averted at the end of the week. Yet the belief probably persists, at least among those who do not live in the depressing atmosphere of fruitless negotiation, that an immediate stoppage would be so monstrous a folly, so futile, and, at worst, so premature as to be unthinkable. Still less is it possible to conceive that the country may be involved in anything of the nature of a general strike. Yet not only are these things on the cards, but there is little beyond instinctive belief in the latent sanity of most Englishmen to nurse the hope that they will not come to pass. Little is known of what has happened during the private meetings of the last few days, mostly held at the summons of the Prime Minister, and still less, of course, of the inner councils of the two parties to the dispute. But the accounts which have been published give the clear impression of indecisiveness and mis-direction. The negotiations, in fact, seem never to have recovered from the initial twist given to them during the preliminary stages of discussion between the owners and the men. It was natural that the owners should have emphasised those aspects of the Report which pleased them most, but it was a mistake from every point of view when the miners followed them into virtual disregard of the constructive proposals of the Report and concentrated on resistance to wage cuts, longer hours, and district settlements. In fact, the early negotiations never really got beyond discussion of the last of the points. With the subsidy coming to an end the owners were forced to post notices and to define their new wage offer, the effect of which was inevitably to force attention still farther away from the broader problems of the industry and to obliterate the carefully drawn perspective of the Report.

When Mr. Baldwin began his efforts at mediation it was his clear policy to extricate the negotiations from the rut in which they had become embedded and to start them afresh on the lines of the Report. Whether he made the attempt or not he does not appear to have succeeded. So far as is known, the discussions have still centred round the three original issues, which, taken by themselves, are probably incapable of adjustment by consent. The latest variation is the offer, which the owners are understood to have in mind, of less drastic cuts in wages, an eight-hour day, and a national settlement of the minimum wage. If the offer is made it will almost certainly be refused. It may be good propaganda, but is not likely to be any more acceptable to the men than the original offer. It would be something substantial if the owners could be induced to

3

waive their demand for district settlements unconditionally. The miners would then be forced to declare their hand and to say whether they would contemplate a reduction of wages under any circumstances at all. Under the pressure of the Trade Unions Congress Committee it is hardly possible that they would continue completely inflexible. But all Mr. Baldwin's efforts to get the owners to withdraw their insistence on district settlements seem only to have produced a vague and unsubstantial offer to make it a bargaining counter in any general settlement which may be reached. It is a disappointing result. Whether anything can be expected from the members of the district mining associations, with whom he is conferring as we write, it is impossible to say. But the main difficulty is not one of personalities but of facts. The economic facts of the industry are such that no terms acceptable to the men are apparently discoverable unless sweetened, as the Commissioners insist that they should be, by the adoption 'of all practicable means for improving its organisation and increasing its efficiency.'

It may be that this point is better understood by the Industrial Commmittee of the Trade Union Congress than it is by any of the other parties concerned in the negotiations. This body, as in the last days of July, is again coming into the forefront of the dispute. It is probably the most effective lever for peace to which the Government can turn. On the other hand, it holds over the head of the country an unmistakable sword. There could be no greater injustice than to regard it as a fomenter of strife. Nobody, probably, is more sincerely anxious for a settlement of the dispute than are the trade union leaders of whom it is composed. On the other hand, unless they can be convinced that the miners have been put in the wrong they will stand by them. The resolution which the committee passed yesterday is mild and reasonable. It contains no suggestion of a threat. It asks only for a suspension of notices and a continuance of negotiations. But if the notices are not withdrawn and the stoppage occurs the Government will have to reckon with the fact that the Committee has not been convinced that the miners have been put in the wrong and that, accordingly, a general refusal by the unions to handle the coal supplies of the country may be attempted. Whether the Trade Unions Congress has the right to hold the country to ransom is not, for the moment in question. The practical question is whether the ransom demanded is reasonable. So far as can be gathered the attitude of the committee is that held by a great number of other people — that reconstruction of the industry ought to be brought firmly into the outlines of any settlement which is proposed and that the objections of the owners to a national settlement of the minimum wage ought to be modified or withdrawn in the light of the recommendations made in the Report. If this is a correct description of the views of the Committee they are worth attention even at the eleventh hour.

OUR LONDON CORRESPONDENT

By private wire

London, Friday Night.

THE GOVERNMENT'S EMERGENCY ARRANGEMENTS

The Government completed all their preparations during the day for applying the provisions of the Emergency Powers Act if a state of emergency should have to be proclaimed. The special constabulary were warned. The Civil Commissioners left for their areas.

These commissioners will exercise the powers of the Executive, that is, of the Government, in their respective areas, and will act on there own responsibility except in decisions of great importance.

If a state of emergency should be proclaimed, the Government will take over the management of broadcasting from the British Broadcasting Company, as they have the power to do under the terms of the company's contract. They will thus have the means of disseminating news by wireless set — an arrangement which might be of considerable importance in case there should be, a printers strike as well as a strike of railwaymen, transport workers, and probably electricians.

The organisation for the maintenance of supplies, a volunteer body formed with Government approval, has been very busy. Its function is to prepare a register of volunteer workers of various qualifications, and when they have prepared it to hand it over to the Government who will make use of it.

Milk and essential services will be the first things to which the Transport Department of the Government's emergency arrangements will give their attention. It may be recalled that the navy and army between them in these days of mechanical warfare have a very large number of technicians, engineers, mechanics, and special workers of all kinds.

EAST HAM

The surprising thing in the East Ham election is that, while the Labour and Liberal votes remain much as at the general election, the Conservative vote has dropped by about 2,000. The fact that East Ham is one of the few eastern areas where there is a large lower middle-class vote has always given the Tories a chance there. It looks as though these East Ham Conservatives are displeased with Mr. Baldwin over the coal subsidy. In these East

5

End boroughs Labour has become very powerful, and what is known as Poplarism is firmly entrenched. The decline in the Tory vote suggests that the East Ham season-ticket holder is losing faith in the Baldwin Government as his guardian against the raids of the Labour municipalities on the rates.

From the first it seemed more than likely that Miss Lawrence would win back the seat, which was only lost to Labour owing to the anti-Bolshevik scare at the general election. She is popular, well known as a worker in social reform, and will be a valuable addition to the Labour ranks in the House of Commons. Miss Lawrence herself explains her success as due to disgust at the raiding of the insurance-funds and 'the driving of the unemployed on the rates.'

p.11

HOPEFUL TURN LATE LAST NIGHT
Truce Proposal to the Miners

PREMIER'S FINAL EFFORTS FOR PEACE
Government Prepare for State of Emergency

The suspense of the past forty-eight hours reached its climax of intensity last night as the minutes remaining before the threatened calamity slipped away without any hopeful sign from Westminster, where Mr. Baldwin and his colleagues, the miners' and the trade union leaders, and the mine-owners' representatives had spent the greater part of the day and night.

Early in the evening the Ministry of Health had issued to local authorities the details of the Government's plans for dealing with the situation should a state of emergency be reached, with the list of Ministers who would act as civil commissioners in each area into which the country is divided up under the emergency scheme, and the King had returned to London for a Privy Council called in connection with the crisis.

The owners' wages and hours offer put before Mr. Baldwin earlier in the day, and modified at the Premier's suggestion, involved the suspension of the eight-hour day, and it was turned down after very little discussion by the miners' delegate conference.

The discussions between Mr. Baldwin and the Industrial Committee at the House of Commons last evening, it is understood, led to a further conditional proposal to the miners for a temporary truce.

Peace at last?
In the afternoon Sir Austen Chamberlain had spoken publicly of the situation as very serious, and it was not until after nine o'clock

last night that there was any hopeful indication. At 9.30 Mr. Ramsay MacDonald declared the situation to be more hopeful.

At ten o'clock last night our political correspondent learned that the situation seemed very hopeful. All through the evening the miners' delegate conference members and the delegates representing 900 unions affiliated to the Trade Unions Congress had remained within call of their conference halls.

From various districts, including Lancashire and Yorkshire, it was reported last night that the ten o'clock shift had not gone down the mines.

OUTLOOK HOPEFUL AT 10 P.M.

(From our Political Correspondent)

London, Friday, 10 p.m.

By ten o'clock in the evening the negotiations had reached a very hopeful position. Success was indeed almost in sight, and only a slight doubt or hesitation on the part of the miners as to a detail in the interpretation of conditions prevented them from agreeing to terms upon which Mr. Baldwin was able to guarantee a suspension of the notices.

REJECTED OWNERS' OFFER

From our Labour Correspondent

London, Friday night

The final break lies now on hours. Last night the coalowners tentatively mentioned their offer, and this morning when the representatives of all the district committees of the Mining Association had arrived in London they confirmed it. They were willing to waive their demand for district minimum and to offer the minimum of the 1921 agreement — 20 per cent on the 1914 standard as against the present 33⅓ per cent, providing that the Seven Hours Act was suspended and eight hours was worked.

Under Mr. Baldwin's pressure the offer was modified. He suggested, and the owners agreed,

That the Seven Hours Act should be suspended until December 31, 1929.

That before that date a committee or commission should be set up to review the economic condition of the industry and the effect of the reorganisation scheme and recommend whether there should be a continuation of the eight hour day, a reduction to 7½ hours, or a return to seven hours.

This offer the miners' conference unanimously rejected.

At the miners' delegate conference Mr. J. McGurk, on behalf of Lancashire, moved the rejection of the owners' offer, and Yorkshire and South Wales supported.

The Prime Minister received the coal-owners' new proposals at noon. He handed them to the Industrial Committee of the Trade Unions Congress and the Miners' Executive. At three they were conveyed to the miners' delegate conference and unanimously rejected after only a few moments' discussion. The Executive representatives − Mr. W.P. Richardson, Mr. S.O. Davies, and Mr. F. Hall, who presented them − conveyed the decision to the Prime Minister in time for the Cabinet meeting which followed at four.

The Industrial Committee and the Miners' Executive remained at the House of Commons, where the coal-owners' executive also arrived. Mr. Baldwin saw all three sides after the Cabinet meeting.

The miners' delegate conference assembled at the Kingsway Hall, first at nine, then at 10.45, at 2.30, at 6.30, and finally stood by until late in the evening.

The conference of trade union executives − met at the Memorial Hall, Farringdon Street, at eleven, at three, at six, at seven, and at 8.30. Many of the delegates did not leave the hall, but sang choruses and smoked and talked.

KING'S RETURN TO LONDON

Special Privy Council

The King arrived at Buckingham Palace shortly after five o'clock yesterday evening, having motored back from Newmarket, instead of going direct to Windsor. It was understood that he would hold a Privy Council to deal with matters arising out of the coal situation.

The King had received a request to hold a Privy Council yesterday evening, and at once replied that he would call in London on his way back from Newmarket. Attended by Colonel Wigram and Major Reginald Seymour, he reached the Palace just after five o'clock. The Privy Council was held at 5.30, the Home Secretary being among the Ministers present, and just before 6.30 the King and the two equerries left to resume their journey to Windsor.

CIRCULAR 636.

Outline of Emergency Plans

WIDE POWERS

Circular 636, to which reference is made in the Ministry of Health's circular to local authorities issued last night, was circulated last November. It opens with the declaration that 'while it is desirable that Government authorities, whether central or local, should keep aloof from any industrial dispute so far as it affects only the employers and the employed in the industry concerned, it is essential that other members of the community should be protected from the dangers and inconveniences arising from it.' This protection can best be supplied by decentralised organisation designed to cause the maintenance of services essential to the well-being of the community.'

The organisation which the Government propose is designed to supplement and to assist in an emergency the normal methods of communication, supply, and distribution, and to give to all those who can help an opportunity of doing so in the manner most required. It is not intended that the Government should substitute new machinery for that ordinarily existing to meet the essential needs of the community.

The circular proceeds to outline the proposed steps under the following heads:–

Civil Commissioners

1. A Minister will in such an emergency act as Civil Commissioner on behalf of the Government in each of ten divisions covering the whole of England and Wales. He will be assisted by a staff consisting mainly of representatives of the departments of Government concerned and dealing with the following subjects – Transport, food, postal services, coal. It will be the duty of the Civil Commissioner and his staff during the emergency to keep in touch with the local authorities in each division and to be available for consultation by them, and he will be empowered if necessary to give decisions on behalf of the Government.

Local Recruiting

2. Each division is divided into suitable areas for administering essential national services and, if considered necessary, for recruiting volunteers for those purposes. In each area there will on an emergency be a local food officer, a local road officer, and a haulage committee and a coal emergency officer, besides representatives (where required) for other essential services.

Feeding the Population

3. On an emergency arising reliance will be placed to the utmost extent upon normal channels for the supply and distribution of food. In the event of any shortage or delay in the supply of essential foodstuffs to the division, the food representatives will be in possession of information as to alternative sources of supply and the means to make them available.

Commandeering Transport

4. Road transport will be dealt with on similar lines. The Road Commissioner upon the Civil Commissioner's staff will be assisted by road officers and haulage committees in each of the areas comprised in the division, who will endeavour by voluntary arrangement to promote the economical use of existing vehicles, and where necessary, the diversion of vehicles from less to more important services.

Coal Rations

5. In an emergency full directions will be sent to the supply and distribution of coal. These directions may, if necessary, limit the supply of coal obtainable for any household or business, and may also place upon local authorities responsibilities for regulating the consumption of gas and electricity within their districts.

Special Constabulary

6. The maintenance of law and order and the protection of persons and property from violence may be one of the most important services. The organisation of the necessary arrangements and the control of the police and special constabulary rest with the police authorities and the Chief Constables, but the local authorities might co-operate, for instance, in securing able-bodied citizens of good character to serve as special constables. The arrangements for the enrolment of special constables will be made by the police, and any men who come forward as special constables or who offer their services in a general capacity and appear most suited for service as special constables should be referred to the police station or other place of enrolment appointed for the purpose.

The breakdown of the negotiations on the night of April 30 was caused by disagreement on the interpretation assigned to the word 'initiated'. The Industrial Committee with MacDonald and Arthur Henderson had agreed a peace formula with Baldwin based upon the withdrawal of lockout notices, the continuation of the subsidy, and the agreement of the miners to consider immediate wage reductions alongside long-term reform. This compromise, however, was rejected by Herbert Smith, who insisted that reorganisation proposals be agreed before wage reductions were implemented. J.H. Thomas' account of the breakdown to the Trade Union Executives' conference reflected his bitter disappointment. The Government, however, in anticipation of such a state of affairs had persuaded the King to call a meeting of the Privy Council to declare a State of Emergency.

The following day (May 1) the trade union movement voted overwhelmingly to begin a selective strike at midnight on Monday May 3. While strike orders were to be issued by individual unions, the 'conduct of the dispute' was formally handed over to the General Council of the TUC. Negotiations with the Government were not, however, broken off and during Saturday evening and most of Sunday the Industrial Committee continued to search for a formula with the Government to avert the strike.

NO LONDON 'DAILY MAIL' TO-DAY

The Press Association received late last night the following communication from the editor of the 'Daily Mail' (London):–

The 'Natsopas' (National Society of Operative Printers and Assistants) at Carmelite House took exception to the leading article which had been prepared for publication in the 'Daily Mail,' Monday, May 3, under the heading, 'For King and Country,' and demanded that alterations should be made by the editor, who refused to comply. They were supported by the machine managers, the stereotypers, and the packers.

Several unions, including the compositors, the process workers, and the telegraphists, declared that it was not within their province to discuss the policy of the newspaper, and resolved to carry on their work. The 'Natsopas' and the members of the unions supporting them ceased work, and consequently there will be no issue of the 'Daily Mail' from Carmelite House this (Monday) morning.

The Daily Mail 'incident' was at the centre of the controversy surrounding the breaking off of negotiations. The Government subsequently claimed that the NATSOPA action, although unofficial, was 'provocative' and forced the Cabinet to take a firm stance against trade union anarchy.

CABINET ULTIMATUM

DEMAND FOR WITHDRAWAL OF GENERAL STRIKE THREAT
Condition of Further Negotiations

DOWNING STREET DISCUSSIONS BREAK DOWN
AT 12 30 A.M.
Railway and Transport Men to Come Out To-morrow

Early this morning, after further futile negotiations which had lasted through the night, the Government issued the following ultimatum to the trade unions:-

The following decision of his Majesty's Government has been conveyed to-night to Mr. Pugh, chairman of the Trade Unions Congress:-

His Majesty's Government believes that no solution of the

difficulties in the coal industry which is both practicable and honourable to all concerned can be reached except by sincere acceptance of the Report of the Commission.

In the expression "acceptance of the Report" is included both the reorganisation of the industry, which should be put in hand immediately and, pending the results of the reorganisation being attained, such interim adjustment of wages or hours of work as will make it economically possible to carry on the industry in the meantime.

If the miners, or the Trade Union Committee on their behalf, were prepared to say plainly that they accept this proposal the Government would have been ready to resume the negotiations and to continue the subsidy for a fortnight.

But since the discussions which have taken place between Ministers and members of the T.U.C. it has come to the knowledge of the Government not only that specific instructions have been sent (under the authority of the executives of trade unions represented at the conference convened by the General Council of the Trade Unions Congress) directing their members in several of the most vital industries and services of the country to carry out a general strike on Tuesday next, but that overt acts have already taken place, including gross interference with the freedom of the press.

Such action involves a challenge to the constitutional rights and freedom of the nation. His Majesty's Government therefore, before it can continue negotiations, must require from the T.U.C. both a repudiation of the actions referred to that have already taken place and an immediate and unconditional withdrawal of the instructions for a general strike.

Mr. Thomas and Mr. Cook each spoke as they came away from Downing Street of "war having been declared".

THE WEEK-END NEGOTIATIONS

The renewal of discussions came after Saturday's decision by the conference of 200 trade union executives to take general strike action in support of the miners, "the first line" of unions to come out to-morrow morning. Following this decision the General Council of the Trade Unions Congress wrote to Mr. Baldwin informing him that they had now taken over from the miners the conduct of the dispute.

The Premier invited explanations of the letter, and from eight on Saturday night to 1 20 yesterday morning there were meetings at Downing Street. Yesterday morning, after further trade union consultations, those Miners' Executive members who had left London were hurriedly recalled.

Mr. Baldwin presided at a Cabinet meeting at noon yesterday, and at five o'clock a further meeting of the Cabinet was

12

held. Communications passed with the trade union leaders, and at nine o'clock last night the Negotiating Committee of the Trade Unions Congress were called to Downing Street, the full General Council and members of the Miners' Executive being summoned later for consultation.

A "state of emergency" was declared on Saturday by Royal proclamation, and orders have been issued for the rationing of coal.

The trade unions have offered to run food trains and organise food distribution, but it is highly unlikely that if a general strike comes the Government would accept such an offer.

The chief industries which are to be closed down to-morrow by the strike call are the railways and other forms of transport.

The collapse of negotiations between the Industrial Committee and the Cabinet at 1.20 a.m. on Monday May 3 came as a complete surprise to the TUC. Baldwin's decision to break off negotiations and demand the unconditional termination of the strike was to be the subject of intense debate throughout the following ten days.

p.8

STOP-PRESS NEWS

T.U.C. REPLY TO GOVERNMENT

The T.U.C. General Council this morning sent to the Prime Minister a letter stating that they had received the Government's decision to terminate discussion with surprise and regret.

'The negotiations which had taken place had been adjourned for a brief period in order to allow the Industrial Committee to confer with the full General Council and the representatives of the Miners' Federation, who were on your premises in order to advance the efforts which the Industrial Committee had persistently been making to accomplish a speedy and honourable settlement of the mining dispute.

The trade union representatives were astounded to learn that without any warning renewed conversations, which it was hoped might pave the way to the opening up of full and unfettered negotiations, had been abruptly terminated by the Government for the reasons stated in your communication.

As to the first reason – instructions to cease work – it is nothing unusual for workmen to cease work in defence under the circumstances as wage-earners, and the specific reason for the decision is to secure the workers the same right as employers insist upon with their workers – namely, that negotiations should be conducted free from the atmosphere of strikes or lock-outs.'

13

The letter disclaims any knowledge of any incident relating to interference with the freedom of the press. Such incidents were distinctly forbidden in their official instructions.

The reply goes on to deplore the wrecking of the T.U.C.'s sincere efforts to an honourable settlement by what is termed the Government's 'unprecedented ultimatum.'

The reply is timed 3 30 a.m.

p.9

THE CASUS BELLI.
Cabinet's Belated Challenge.

TO-DAY'S DEBATE.
Question Labour is to Raise.

(From our Political Correspondent.)

London, Monday Morning

There is an astonishing inconsistency in the Government's statement of their reason for breaking off the negotiations, finally and fatally, this morning.

The Trade Unions Congress announced the general strike at noon on Saturday, and conveyed the decision to the Government at once. The same evening, in spite of that, negotiations were taken up again where they had been broken off on Friday night. They were continued all yesterday, and carried into the small hours of this morning. Now the Government turn round and say that the order of a general strike involves a challenge to the constitutional rights and freedom of the nation, and that they cannot continue negotiations unless there is an immediate and unconditional withdrawal of the instructions for a general strike.

How is the constitutional situation different in that respect to-day from what it was on Saturday noon? True a single union, entirely on its own account, stopped the publication of a newspaper this morning. Is it pretended that that was the last straw? These questions will assuredly be raised in the House of Commons this afternoon when the whole tragic affair will come up for debate.

There is another story behind this last breakdown. The official explanation will not do. This, of course, is not to deny the perfect correctness of the Government's statement of the constitutional issue, but it could have waited another precious day.

THE HOME SECRETARY.

Sir William Joynson-Hicks, Home Secretary, speaking at the Royal Academy banquet on Saturday night, said that surely that unselfishness which caused men to sacrifice all that they held dear for the sake of their country in the Great War will lead them once more to obey the call of their country to sacrifice on both sides of what they deem to be their rights in order to preserve peace in our land.

'That is the object of his Majesty's Ministers. That is the purpose to which they have been devoting themselves for the last few weeks. But if it be that strife has to come, if it be that there is to be an economic dispute, then I pray that the dispute may be conducted with friendliness, in amity, and, above all, that it may not widen its borders until it is not an economic but a political dispute. At all events I can say to you that one of the great functions of any Government is to preserve law and order, which is the heritage of every man in this land from the highest to the lowest place. This obligation is paramount in the minds of his Majesty's Ministers, and will be carried out by them with unflinching determination, and, I believe, with the assent and co-operation of all men loyal to their King and country.'

"THE COUNTRY MUST BE PREPARED."
Home Secretary's Notice.

RECRUITING TO-DAY.

The following notification by the Home Secretary, and issued from the Deputy Chief Civil Commissioner's office, was made late last night:-

Although discussions are still proceeding, in view of the action of the Trade Unions Congress the country must be prepared for a general strike in many industries and public services on Monday night.

The Government has taken all steps to maintain the supply of food, fuel, light, and power, and to ensure the protection of all engaged in these services, and the preservation of law and order.

Recruiting stations for volunteers will be opened to-morrow, and loyal citizens should hold themselves in readiness to assist the Government.

Full information will be issued to-morrow, but in the event of any difficulty occurring in finding the right office on Tuesday inquiries should be made at the nearest police station.

THE TRADE UNIONS' DECISION.
A Sombre Mood.

MR. MACDONALD'S ELOQUENCE.
Miners' Leader's Offer.

(From our Labour Correspondent.)

London, Sunday.

In the small hours of Saturday morning the general secretaries of nearly 200 unions received the general strike proposals. After a few hours of sleep the members of their executives were called together in groups and decisions taken on whether they were ready to act on the proposals.

At noon the full conference assembled and a roll call of the unions was taken. Unions with 3,653,527 members accepted the policy of the General Council; unions with 49,911 members dissented; unions with 319,000 members also affiliated to the Congress were not present. Some of the unions were not able yesterday to pledge absolutely their executives, but they will be consulted before Monday. The dissentients were not important. The great mass of the trade unions swung into line.

The conference then adjourned for a little while so that the General Council might prepare its plans. On re-assembling it was opened to the press, and Mr. Ernest Bevin announced the general strike. Certain "vital trades and staple trades" had been selected to begin the strike. No worker called out in these trades must go to work after the night shift on Monday night or on Tuesday morning. There must be no quibbling, no argument. "You must take your orders and obey them, believing that those who are charged with the responsibility of guiding will exercise the best guidance they can." There was to be a "voluntary service to ensure the feeding of the people." Essential foodstuffs were to be "organised under a voluntary arrangement by the trade unions."

Mr. Bevin was short and businesslike. Mr. Bromley followed and pledged the locomotive men who, with the transport and railwaymen of Mr. Bevin's and Mr. Thomas's union, would bear the brunt of the stoppage.

The miners' case was put by Mr. Herbert Smith in a speech which breathed no defiance, only sadness that things should have come to such a pass. He emphasised, and repeated his emphasis, his offer to the Government that the miners would go all through the Commission's report and accept the outcome of the negotiations, providing they were not asked in advance to say that they would accept wages reductions.

16

The mood of the conference was best summed up by Mr. MacDonald in one of the most difficult as it was one of the most moving and eloquent speeches of his career. He said little or nothing of the general strike – his opinion of it would probably not bear expression. His words were addressed to the Government and to the wider public outside to compel the Government to re-open negotiations, to begin where it had left off the night before, and to accomplish what might have been accomplished had only a few hours more grace been given. He stressed Mr. Smith's offer again and again.

But it would be wrong to read into the offers of conciliation that ran through the speeches the inference that the conference was merely bluffing. As the delegates went away, each with his plan of organisation, one could hear them say: "Well, we're all in it. We've got to go through with it."

RELUCTANCE, NOT EXULTATION.

The Continent will note that the declaration came on May Day, and the hearts of the Communists are already rejoicing at the auspicious synchronism with the cardinal date of the revolutionary calendar. But any such feeling was quite absent from the conference. It had intensity, a curious thrill of adventure, but lacked absolutely any exultation. It was as though an army of martyrs were going out very reluctantly, almost sacrificially, to battle. A placing of the unions' "all on the altar of our great movement," Mr. Bevin called it. There can rarely have been in the history of Labour a more revolutionary decision taken with so little hope and so little fervour. The Communists and the theoretical advocates of "mass action" were left far behind; British Labour entered on a perilous path under the command of a Socialist ex-Prime Minister, a non-Socialist ex-Cabinet Minister, and two "moderate" trade union leaders, Mr. Pugh and Mr. Bevan. A new chapter must be added to the history of the vagaries of the British political temperament.

p.12

MR. J.R. CLYNES.
Stoppage that Can Solve Nothing.

Mr. J.R. Clynes, M.P., speaking at Melksham on Saturday, said Mr. Baldwin had no doubt tried his best to get the parties to agree, but if a well thought out policy on the part of the Government in relation to coal had been as ready and as perfect as preparations appeared to be for dealing with the stoppage a stoppage could assuredly have been averted. It might be that Mr. Baldwin had a plan. If so there should be no waiting until after a dispute had started to reveal it.

There is no instance where such a continued opportunity for settlement has been offered to a Government. This is no case of a sudden attack on the part of the workers. The miners are attacking nobody. From the moment the Coal Commission concluded its labours the Cabinet should have acted, because the State has for good or ill become the custodian of the nation's interests in relation to the coal trade. There is no occupation to which the nation is more closely linked and if in this industry a living wage with fair, human conditions cannot be afforded to the miners the nation will turn to the alternative of national control and ownership in a basic industry.

From my knowledge of the inside work of negotiation I can say that the whole of the trade unions concerned have maintained a consistent and temperate endeavour to secure a fairly reasonable settlement, and they may remain confident of a public unwillingness to drive the miners to a lower level than for a long time they have had to endure because of past wage reductions. The public should not forget that on the men's part this is not a strike. The stoppage is due to the mineowners refusing to withdraw notices of lock-out unless mine workers submit to new conditions which would place them on a wage level, so far as many are concerned, far below the level of pre-war pay. Men who have done their duty by the nation are entitled to the sympathy of the nation expressed in its most practical form.

The stoppage can be of no service. All the problems will be left to settle after work is resumed. Neither strike nor lock-out can at this stage assist the coal industry in any effort to overcome the difficulties of the trade. The owners therefore should have been checked from taking any step which would only deepen the trouble in the coal industry.

It was significant that Clynes was at pains to point out that the dispute was purely about the conditions of work and rates of pay in the mining industry. The Labour Party was anxious at all costs to play down any suggestion that the trade union movement was challenging the constitutional authority of the Government as suggested in the account of the Home Secretary's speech delivered on May 1.

THE GENERAL STRIKE PLANS.
'First Line' Unions to Stop Work To-morrow.

GOVERNMENT AND VICTUALLING OFFERS.

(From our Labour Correspondent.)

London, Sunday.

The general strike plans as presented in rough outline to the Trade Unions Conference yesterday provided for the stoppage of all forms of transport (including docks and railways), printing trades (including the newspapers), the iron and steel, metal and heavy chemical trades, the building trade (apart from housing and hospital work), and electricity and gas supply for power. The power to call the unions out is vested in the General Council. It is announced to-night that instructions for a stoppage on Monday night have been sent to the unions in the transport, press, iron and steel, metal and heavy chemicals, engineering, and building trades. Last night Mr. C.T. Cramp sent the following telegram to all branches of the National Union of Railwaymen:–

Executive Committee instruct all our members not to take duty after Monday next. Arrangements to be made locally so that all men will finish their term of duty at their home station on Tuesday morning.

The other railway unions have issued similar instructions, and the N.U.R. has sent circulars to its branches asking them 'to make the thing a success.'

In his speech announcing the procedure, Mr. Bevan added the following explanatory note:–

We have not definitely fixed a time by an hour or so because of local difficulties with regard to finishing time. Railwaymen must necessarily be immediately involved, but because of the difficulty of getting home we will arrange their consideration to come within the scope of our immediate arrangements, but transport workers and all those engaged in the vital services will not start work on Tuesday morning.

Other trades will finish shifts as and when they are required to do so by practice.

There is no suggestion that the cotton operatives should be called out early. They were asked yesterday to stand by ready to act if called on. They, like the members in other manufacturing industries, would be affected soon enough by a shortage of coal.

19

A serious crop of problems arises over the General Council's proposal that the unions should 'do everything in their power to organise the distribution of milk and food to the whole of the population.' For this purpose food trains are to be allowed, and every opportunity is to be taken 'to ensure that food, milk, medical and surgical supplies' are efficiently provided to hospitals and schools.

The railway and transport unions met at Eccleston Square this morning to discuss their plans. If a strike does occur the Government will take no cognisance of this unofficial attempt to victual the people and to take over the functions of Government. It will act through its Civil Commissioners and not through any body of trade unionists. It would be competent for a commissioner to take over, for instance, the co-operative stores and appoint the manager as his officer. In that case it is possible the co-operative employees might be called out.

But this side of the strike plans is all very vague, and the General Council have probably very little idea of where their proposals would lead them.

p.12

MR. SMITH REPORTS TO THE MINERS.
The Pact with the T.U.C.

NO DISORDERS APPEAL.

After being in session for two and a half hours on Saturday morning the Miners' Delegate Conference at the Kingsway Hall adjourned at 11 30 to enable the full Executive of the Miners' Federation to consult with the T.U.C. at the noon conference of unions. The miners' delegates had heard and approved the proposals for united action which were to be laid before the conference of unions, and a strong appeal to the men in the districts to refrain from any action which would cause any disturbance.

It was three o'clock when Mr. Smith and Mr. Cook reached Kingsway Hall to convey to the miners' delegates the result of the proceedings at the T.U.C. meeting. Press representatives were admitted to the meeting to hear Mr. Smith's address to the delegates.

'This is one of the most important moments in my life,' said Mr. Smith. 'We have got handed over to us to-day guaranteed help, which means conditions of labour and everything, to the extent that 3,653,527 of our colleagues are going to stand by us. In addition 45,911 have not said "No," but there are certain qualifications and consultations to make, and replies in those cases will be given on

Monday morning. Even on the 1st of May, with all this proffered help and loyalty, would to God that we could save this war. Both myself and the Executive have done everything that is possible to get peace. What for? Women and children have got to suffer through this crisis.'

After referring to the terms offered them, Mr. Smith proceeded that, even if their allies had not agreed to support them, the miners would have been compelled to resist them, because once they accepted them they would get back to conditions of slavery. (Cheers.) Under the 1921 agreement they had men working every day possible, and even then they were unable to get a bare subsistence. Over 250,000 of their people every week had received parish pay. (Shame.) Yet they had men like Lord Birkenhead asking 'Are you prepared to give an undertaking to accept a reduction in wages?' When Lord Birkenhead was pressed what was his suggestion – what would he do? When this was put to him he tried to avoid the issue by telling them that he was not there to answer questions. The Government had bungled in this business.

Joint Negotiation Stipulation.

With regard to the crisis, everything will be done to arrive at a settlement, but we are not going to have peace at any price. We have got a clear understanding with the General Council of the T.U.C. that, although we are handing this matter over to them, we must function with them from time to time. Any negotiation must be joint negotiation, and any advice from either side must be considered jointly. We said we are prepared to give everything over except that we are not going to give you our revolver – in other words, our tongue, – we are going to keep that free. 'All we ask you people to do is to meet with us, discuss with us, and meet with the other side if they wish, and take joint part in responsibility,' that is what the General Council said to us in effect.

'I told them we had no hesitation in doing this. We are going to break up this afternoon. I want to advise every man at this meeting to go back to his district and advise his men not to be tempted by people who will be paid spies to cause some little scene, and then to say, "The miners are rioting." If this Government is wise they will keep the guns and soldiers away from mining areas, and make us responsible for good conduct in those areas. (Cheers.) It is possible to egg our men on to a position that they would otherwise never get, and plenty of people are willing to do it. It ought to be our advice to them to say, "Here we are, we have not sought this, we have been forced into this position, we are going to stand by this position with our honest comrades in the movement." '

'This is no firework business,' he added. 'I am going into it fully convinced that I am compelled to do it, and I am going to resist it, as I know you will, to the bitter end.' (Loud cheers.)

The Conference then resumed private sitting, at the end of which no official statement was issued except the announcement that a vote of thanks was passed to Mr. Smith for his address.

p.12

'CLOSING DOWN OF THE PRESS.'
T.U.C. and Wireless News.

In an official statement issued on Saturday night from the headquarters of the General Council of the Trade Union Congress, it is stated:—

In view of the fact that the Government is understood to have commandeered the British Broadcasting Company, and in anticipation of the closing down of the press, the General Council is making arrangements for direct communication with the head offices and branch offices of the affiliated trade unions, and all authoritative statements, reports, and announcements will be made directly to them.

The General Council warns the trade union and labour movement to take no notice of any statement that may be broadcast by wireless or circulated in any other form. General secretaries of the trade unions have already been requested to supply the necessary information to enable direct communications to be maintained.

p.13

EMERGENCY PLANS.
Satisfactory Throughout the Country.

APPEAL TO PUBLIC.

(From our Political Correspondent.)

London, Sunday.

All the preliminary work of putting the emergency control into operation has been completed, and the Government states that it is absolutely satisfactory throughout the country. Food conditions, it is added, are normal. There is no need for any anxiety on the part of the public, still less for any suggestion of panic.

The amenities of the public, it is pointed out, are largely in their own hands. If they carry out loyally and unselfishly the regulations which the Government will issue from time to time with regard to food, petrol, and other supplies, if there is no hoarding and they prepare to face up to the situation, then their own comfort and convenience will be safeguarded. The Government ask for loyal and scrupulous observance of regulations. The Government's view is that there must be a Government, and that it must govern, not as taking sides in the dispute, but as asserting itself as the supreme power of the community which must override all sectional interests.

Distributing Supplies

A suggestion in some periodical that the Government were going to use 'naked force to smash the miners' is resented. As a matter of fact it is declared that the forces of the Government will probably do more to protect the wives and families of the strikers than anybody else. The Government believes that its organisation is working well. It is perfectly well prepared, whatever the event, whether peace or, as it has been rather unhappily called, war. As to practical arrangements, I am informed that if there is a general strike Hyde Park will be closed and reserved as a distributing centre. The trade union offer to distribute supplies and see to equitable distribution is met with the answer that that is for the Government. There is only one authority for the maintenance of order and supplies in each district, and that is the Civil Commissioner who is in each area the Government.

STATE OF EMERGENCY DECLARED.

The Proclamation.

A supplement to the 'London Gazette' of Saturday was issued in the following terms:—

By the King – A Proclamation
GEORGE R.I.

Whereas by the Emergency Powers Act, 1920, it is enacted that if it appears to Us that any action has been taken or is immediately threatened by any persons or body of persons of such a nature and on so extensive a scale as to be calculated, by interfering with the supply and distribution of food, water, fuel, or light, or with the means of locomotion, to deprive the community or any substantial portion of the community, of the essentials of life, We may, by Proclamation, declare that a state of emergency exists:

And whereas the present immediate threat of cessation of work in coal mines does, in Our opinion, constitute a state of emergency within the meaning of the said Act:

Now, therefore, in pursuance of the said Act, We do, by and with the advice of Our Privy Council, hereby declare that a state of emergency exists.

Given at our Court at Buckingham Palace, this 30th day of April, in the year of Our Lord, one thousand nine hundred and twenty-six, and in the sixteenth year of Our Reign.

GOD SAVE THE KING.

AIR SERVICES AS USUAL.

The majority of the employees of Imperial Airways are stated to be non-union men, and all services between London and the Continent will be run as usual in the event of a general strike. Every available Handley-Page Napier air liner is being got ready to supplement the services as required. In addition Imperial Airways will have available several smaller machines for air taxi flights to any part of the British Isles or Europe.

It was understood at Croydon yesterday that should a general strike come Vickers-Napier night bombing-planes of the Royal Air Force may be used for the transport of mails within the British Isles.

p.12

NORTH-WESTERN AREA PREPARATIONS.
Major Hennessy's Statement.

(From our Correspondent.)

Liverpool, Sunday.

Nearly a quarter of a million workers will be affected in the Merseyside area should a general strike come into operation.

Liverpool is the headquarters for the north-western area, extending from Carlisle in the north as far down as Merionethshire, and the Civil Commissioner for this area (Major G. Hennessy, M.P.) arrived in Liverpool yesterday to take charge at the headquarters, 12, St. John's Lane, Liverpool.

During the week-end Major Hennessy, with his staff, was busily engaged in perfecting the organisation for the transport of the necessaries of life. In an interview the Major expressed the hope that the available supplies of coal would not be acquired by those who have large storage capacity and the means wherewith to lay in big stocks of fuel to the disadvantage of others.

'The Government,' he said, 'are not taking sides in the dispute but are merely, as it were, keeping the ring. Our powers are very wide, and if and when the emergency becomes sufficiently grave we will be able to take the necessary steps.'

Sir Arnold Rushton, ex-Lord Mayor of Liverpool, is the Divisional Officer for the north-western area. 'Our organisation exists,' he remarked, 'to assist the trader in case he finds any difficulty in transport in any other way.'

Colonel Tudsbury, the Road Commissioner for the north-western area, states that transport arrangements have been organised all over the territory concerned, so that in the event of any breakdown of the ordinary means of communication they knew where to get the necessary transport facilities.

The Chief Constable of Liverpool (Mr. Lionel D. Everett) gave an assurance that there is no cause for alarm. So far, he said, as the police are concerned, plans have been very carefully laid for the purpose of meeting any emergency which might possibly arise.

For industrial and shipping purposes there are at present good stocks of coal on hand in the Merseyside district, and the Birkenhead and Wallasey Corporations, by whom the ferry services on the Mersey are operated, have such supplies that they can view the situation with equanimity.

p.9.

TROOPS MOVED.
Government's Precautionary Measure.

It was officially announced on Saturday that as a precautionary measure the Government have moved certain detachments of troops into South Wales, Lancashire, and Scotland.

This has been done, it is stated, solely in order that the detachments may be available, should the necessity arise, to assist the police in the maintenance of law and order, and in the protection of life and property.

p.11

NO SOLDIERS FOR MANCHESTER.
Sir Robert Peacock's Statement.

It was reported during the week-end that purely as a precautionary measure troops had been moved into certain industrial areas. One detachment of troops, it was suggested, arrived in Manchester on Saturday.

The Chief Constable of Manchester (Sir Robert Peacock) last night denied that there was any truth in the suggestion that troops had been moved into Manchester. 'There are no troops here,' he said, 'and none will be required.'

Sir Robert added that no steps had been taken in Manchester to augment the special police force. There will be an inspection parade of the existing force on Tuesday next.

LABOUR'S MAY-DAY CELEBRATIONS.
An Overshadowed Affair in London.

FLOOD OF ORATORY IN THE PARK.

(From our London Staff.)

Fleet Street, Saturday.

The gravity of the crisis, overshadowed Labour's May Day celebration in London. The newspaper placards, 'General Strike Ordered,' along the route of the procession made the fiery slogans on the Labour banners look rather foolish. Truth seemed to be beating prophecy. Although this was predominantly a Left-wing rally, the speeches in the park were rather expressive of uneasy excitement than of aggressive confidence.

As May Day fell on a Saturday the procession from the Embankment to the Park was unusually large. Carefully shepherded by police mounted on performing horses – trained not to wink an eyelid under the sudden blare of brass bands – it trailed along the half-deserted streets in the afternoon thick with huge trade union banners that swelled in the wind. The procession seemed to be half a pleasure outing for women and children and half an assertion of strength by the elements in Labour that welcome the prospect of an upheaval with a sort of fearful joy. One saw the dust carts of benevolent Labour municipalities decked with red and full of children singing the 'Red Flag' as Sunday-school children sing hymns on their days out – merely as an excuse for expressing pleasure in life.

Explosive Literature

Their mothers, dressed in the traditional East End black, waved red flags with the same cheerful intent. The mass of the walkers were workmen of the class that has no change of clothes even for a ceremonial occasion. It was an array of caps and scarves, with a sprinkling of smarter artisans and a top-dressing, so to speak, of bourgeois Socialists and Communists. There were young women in 'party' costumes gracefully scattering explosive literature by the way. The official element in trade unionism was not very evident, and the complexion of the procession was so manifestly advanced that the old-fashioned banners, such as the one showing a stiff workman receiving benefits from a paternal union in Victorian surroundings, looked odd over that display of unorthodox red. One or two new banners suggested the welcome growth of an art movement in trade union banners, and there were a few flights of revolutionary fancy, as

26

in the funeral procession 'Imperialism,' symbolised in a mock coffin carried by bearers.

Provocative Fascists.

The thin crowd of spectators on the pavements was either chaffing or mildly interested. There was nothing of what is technically called 'trouble,' although a brake-load of Fascists were stupid enough to parade along past the procession with provocative cries. In the park the women and children wisely devoted themselves to enjoying life as much as the dull and rather cold afternoon would allow. For the men there was speaking from about a dozen platforms, at each of which a cumbrously vague resolution was carried – evidently drafted before the crisis. The big speakers of the Labour party were not present; doubtless they were usefully employed in trying to avert the disaster which was cheerfully welcomed by some irresponsibles in the park.

The demonstration roused no interest in the polite classes, though one noted an immaculate young man of the Guards' officer type fixing his astonished monocle on Mr. Saklatvala at the height of his argument. Mr. Saklatvala seemed to be the hero of the day. He was followed to his platform by a swirling wake of enthusiasts, and his meeting was much the biggest. He is, one imagines, by far the most powerful mob orator of the day. This sallow Indian, with a face worn by fanatical passion, dominated the whole scene as, with outstretched, claw-like hands, he harangued for a good half-hour. With a sort of sombre joy, he acclaimed the general strike as the definite rising of Labour against their oppressors, to a chorus of 'Good old Saklatvala.' The Oriental touch was pronounced. A young Indian had a stand to himself and worked himself into amazing contortions of excitement. A party of Lascar seamen were in Mr. Saklatvala's audience and watched him with expressionless faces of old ivory. They seemed to be wondering what it was all about as they shivered in their thin garments. In the pauses of speech the whirring of kinema cameras made itself heard, but the camera men were rewarded by no 'scenes' and one's impression of the crowd was that there was no mischief in it.

For further details of Saklatvala see 'Details of the Main Characters'.

CITY LABOUR DAY DEMONSTRATION.
Mr. Compton, M.P., on the Strike.

'NO TIME FOR CHEERS.'

It was a dreary May Day procession that marched, under dripping banners and rain-sodden umbrellas, from Ardwick Green to Belle Vue on Saturday. Men and women in gleaming macintoshes and wearing the red and yellow favours of the Labour party; delegates from the trade unions following in dignity behind their banners; Communists with broad ribbons across their shoulders – a splash of scarlet in the drab train; hatless youths carrying sheaves of literature; groups of decorated children – a quarter-mile procession crawling like a spiritless snake along the dampness of Hyde Road. Here and there along the line were tableaux mounted upon carts and lorries; blindfolded Justice, her wet robes clinging to her limbs, a 'bloated capitalist,' with one hand on a soda syphon and the other gripping the rope which ended in a noose around a workman's neck. The banners of the trade unions were varied by those of other groups, ranging from a sober 'stand by the miners' to the appeal of the Communists – 'Don't shoot the workers.'

'What's all this?' asked a man in the line of spectators along the street.

'I think it's some Labour thing,' came a woman's answer.

Galvanised to Enthusiasm.

Banners and tableaux, raincoats and umbrellas passed through the double gates into Belle Vue gardens. There, packed into the great hall, the 'labour thing,' suddenly became a tense, unified personality. The words that galvanised it to enthusiasm, almost, to passion, were those of Mr. Joe Compton, M.P.: 'The trade unions of the country have decided to call a general strike.'

For a fraction of a second the audience was hushed and the wail of an infant could be heard at the back of the hall. Then a wild burst of cheering broke out. The Communists waved their red streamers and hats were thrown into the air. Thereafter every reference from the platform to 'the coming fight' and every appeal to 'stand by the miners' was received with cheers and applause. The solidarity of the meeting was incontestable.

Weapon of Starvation.

Mr. Compton spoke of the gravity of the situation, which might turn out to be the greatest industrial crisis the world had ever known. 'This is no time for cheers,' he said, 'but a time for cool heads, calm intellects, and determination.' The deliberate threat of starvation was hanging over the miners and their families. The coalowners, in his opinion, were determined to have a continuation of the subsidy, by which they had been getting money for nothing. The first responsibility for this great upheaval rested with the owners, but there was also behind the Prime Minister on his own benches in Parliament a gang which was determined to have a scuffle with the workers. 'They have thrown down the challenge and, by Heaven, we have picked it up!' (Applause.)

Mr. Compton asked his audience to show in no uncertain voice that they were determined that this 'damnable, brutal, cowardly weapon of starvation' should not be held over the miners' heads. 'You will be faced with difficulties even in the streets,' he warned. 'The paid agents of the capitalist system will be out again to put obstacles in the way of the workers.' Someone in the front row made a disparaging reference to Mr. Thomas. 'I wish some of you had an opportunity of seeing Thomas as a negotiator,' answered Mr. Compton. 'Then we should not hear so many of these sarcastic remarks. Thomas has worked like a Trojan for his class, and if the fight comes Jimmy Thomas will be found on the side of his people.'

Mr. J.E. Sutton, M.P., chairman of the meeting, appealed to the workers in every industry to take up the fight for the miners. If the miners had to fight alone he believed there were stocks of coal sufficient for three months, but if the transport, railway, and other workers would only take the side of the miners then he believed the Government would be brought to its knees.

A long resolution (evidently framed before the last swift developments of the situation) contained the paragraph:– 'We pledge ourselves, especially in this time of crisis, to support in every way, by every means in our power, the mineworkers of this country in their just resistance to the intolerable demands of the mineowners. We declare that this struggle is not a miners' struggle alone. He who is not for the miners is against the working class.' This was carried with acclamation.

p.12

FOREIGN ECHOES OF THE CRISIS.
Sterling Down in New York.

(Reuter's Telegram.)

New York, Saturday.

The decision in regard to a general strike in vital services in Great Britain is held responsible for the irregular opening of the stock market this morning, the recent bullish enthusiasm being dampened. There was selling of sterling, the demand rate dropping 3-16th of a cent. Cotton and other markets were also influenced adversely. The coal market was buoyant in expectation of higher prices and a better demand for the American product if an early settlement of the strike is not reached. In shipping quarters an upward revision of charter rates is also foreseen.

All the evening newspapers feature the news of the coal stoppage and its attendant perils. The more sensational of them proclaim, for example: 'Dictator Rule of Britain in Strike: Troops Rushed to Mine Areas' or 'Martial Law Status Proclaimed in Britain.' The massive headlines and the make-up of several newspapers are very reminiscent of the days of the Great War.

GENERAL STRIKE TO GO ON.

COMMONS MOVE FAILS.
Fruitless Meeting Between Ministers and Union Leaders.

NOTICES THE STUMBLING-BLOCK.
Start of the Transport Stoppage This Morning.

A last attempt to avert the general strike timed for Monday midnight collapsed within an hour of twelve.

Mr. J.H. Thomas declared as he left the House, "The strike is on," and Mr. Cook said, "They failed; the general strike is on to-morrow." Mr. Baldwin reported the breakdown at a Cabinet meeting at 11 p.m.

Westminster had become the scene of renewed discussions and much excitement about eight o'clock last night during the debate on the Premier's afternoon statement in the House on the industrial crisis.

Mr. Baldwin's speech had been followed by a moderately phrased reply by Mr. J.H. Thomas, as Labour's spokesman. Later Mr. Churchill reiterated that if the strike notices were withdrawn the Government were prepared to continue negotiations.

Mr. Thomas pressed to know whether the withdrawal of lock-out notices was included. Mr. Churchill would not commit himself, but indicated that a reply might be given later, and the Prime Minister, followed by other Ministers, then withdrew, apparently for consultations.

After the close of Mr. Churchill's speech Mr. J.H. Thomas had an interview with the Attorney General. Mr. Thomas afterwards had a short conference with the members of the Miners' Executive, who were meeting in the Committee corridor, and then returned to Sir Douglas Hogg's room.

At 10 20 a joint meeting between the Miners' Executive and the Trade Unions Congress representatives was in progress at the House but it was stated that there had not then been a rapprochement with the Government. Then at 11 p.m. came the news of the final breakdown.

WORKERS WHO ARE TO STOP TO-DAY.

The general strike plans provide for the stoppage to-day of all forms of transport (including docks and railways), printing trades (including the newspapers), the iron and steel, metal, and heavy chemical trades, the building trade (apart from housing and hospital work), and electricity and gas supply for power.

At midnight the Manchester stations were picketed, and though the London trains left it was doubtful whether they would reach their destination. No trams ran in Manchester after midnight.

POINTS FROM COMMONS DEBATE.

The Prime Minister made an important statement on the industrial crisis in the House of Commons yesterday afternoon. Points from the speech follow:—

No settlement had been made of recent years by Government interference which does not contain in it the germs of future trouble.

The Government has always felt the mining industry had to be brought face to face with the problem of supporting itself without a subsidy.

What we wanted to get [in the Saturday night discussions] was an assurance from the T.U.C. Council on behalf of the miners that they really believed that given a fortnight a settlement would be arrived at on the basis of the Coal Report.

I did not feel so hopeful last night, though I determined not to abandon the hope until the last moment.

Time was running out, and do not let anyone forget the risk I was running as Prime Minister in negotiating like that up to the last minute under the threat of a general strike.

At about 11 30 p.m. I learned that certain overt acts had already taken place in anticipation of a general strike — acts perhaps not so grave in themselves, but grave in their signification, interfering with the freedom of the press.

Such actions as these, coupled with the representative unions' instructions, made me realise that we had got to a point when it was impossible for the Government to pursue negotiations.

31

I do not believe there had been anything like a thoroughgoing consultation with the rank and file before this despotic power of ordering a general strike was put into the hands of a small executive in London.

I became convinced last night that Mr. Pugh and those with him who sought peace were not in control and that it would be wrong and dangerous to continue talking until we could get an immediate and unconditional withdrawal of the general strike instructions.

The Government found itself challenged with an alternative government, a government ignorant of the way in which its commands were being carried out and incapable of arresting disobedience.

Statements have been made that there is a general attack on wages in the air. I know of no such movement against wages.

I do not think all the leaders when they assented to a general strike realised that they were threatening ordered government and going nearer to civil war than we have been for centuries.

It is not wages that are in peril, it is the freedom of our Constitution.

So far everything I cared for has been smashed to bits at this moment, but that does not take away from me either my faith or my courage.

MR. J.H. THOMAS.

If the worst comes, and whatever the result may be, the same economic facts will be aggravated, and it is only a blind idiot and a fool who thinks otherwise.

The only thing the General Council of the T.U.C. asks the Prime Minister is to give the negotiators a fair chance, for they cannot conduct negotiations under the threat of a lock-out. Their plea is the withdrawal of the notices.

If a ballot were taken in this country I do not believe 2 per cent would vote for a revolution.

This is not a revolution, it is a plain economic dispute, in which we want justice.

The responsibility to try to save the situation rests upon us all, and it is for Parliament, as representing the people of the country, to try to avert it. A last effort ought to be made.

MR. LLOYD GEORGE.

I am going to make an appeal in Parliament to see if it can avert an unknown catastrophe – to bring the parties to some sort of accommodation.

The declaration of a general strike was a mistake. It was equally a mistake for the Government to break off negotiations.

Would it not be possible now to resume negotiations and for the Government to make it absolutely clear what legislation they were prepared to introduce?

p.9

THE ULTIMATUM MYSTERY.
What was the Explanation of the Sudden Change?

YESTERDAY'S LABOUR EFFORTS.

(From our London Correspondent.)

London, Monday.

In the accounts of the final negotiations between the Trade Unions Congress and the Premier on Sunday there is an important gap according to information that reaches me. The trade union delegates left Downing Street about one o'clock on Sunday morning with a formula from Mr. Baldwin for their consideration. The arrangement was that they were to return at 1 p.m. or 3 p.m. – there seems to have been a misunderstanding as to the time – with their reply. They were sitting in continual session, but as the Miners' Executive had dispersed they could not be got together until much later. The conference went over Mr. Baldwin's formula and, according to what I am told, they decided in the end to accept it with certain alterations.

Under the impression that three o'clock was the stipulated time they had telephoned at 3 30 to Downing Street explaining why they had not been able to come at three and saying they were not yet ready. They were told that there was no hurry. It was not till six o'clock that they were able to go to Downing Street, but when they telephoned that they were ready to come they became aware of a certain change in the official atmosphere.

THE MIDNIGHT CHANGE.

They were asked in the end to come at nine. They went at nine, and three delegates went up to the Premier to apologise for their lateness and say that with certain alterations they were willing to accept the formula. What happened in the conversation with Mr. Baldwin my information does not provide, but it is certain that the delegates went downstairs and worked again on the formula and changed it so that it read as their proposals. They sent for the Miners' Executive and went on with their discussions till about midnight, when Mr. Baldwin sent down for the chairman and secretary of the T.U.C., and after a few words, in which the interference that night with the publication of a London newspaper was mentioned, the Government's ultimatum in typewriting was handed to them, and that terminated the negotiations.

Certain inferences are naturally drawn from these happenings. Between the time that the Premier offered a formula to the delegates and the time when they informed him of their acceptance of it with certain alterations a Cabinet meeting had sat. What occurred upstairs when the delegates presented their reply, as I have said, is not known, but from what happened afterwards it would seem clear that Mr. Baldwin was no longer ready to consider the acceptance of his formula by the T.U.C., but required them to transform it into a proposal of their own and in the end to take up the position expressed in the ultimatum.

The inference is that Mr. Baldwin, not having a reply to his formula to put before the Cabinet meeting and moved by the report of the interference with the press, was then ready to follow the "diehards" of his Cabinet.

p.8

Leader   **THE DAY OF RECKONING.**

By the time these lines are read the country may be in the grip of the most devastating civil conflict of which this generation has had experience. For the moment all argument on its origins is lost in an almost overwhelming sense of its magnitude, the incalculable consequences to which it may lead, and the possibility of discovering, even yet, some loophole for escape. We are a good-natured and tolerant people, but if we permit this strike we put ourselves to a trial which will test the quality of forbearance as even the Great War did not test it. There seem to be, broadly, only two ways of escape – that either the Trade Unions Congress should withdraw its strike orders or that the Government should withdraw its ultimatum. Both are in the wrong. The Trade Unions Congress in ordering over a million men immediately to stop work, most or all of whom can only do so in breach of their agreements, and in selecting those men whose absence from work will most quickly, as it hopes, coerce the Government and country is clearly acting contrary not only to our laws but to the democratic principle of government. If it were successful in this it would have established a powerful precedent for a policy which would at one time or another have to be repudiated, resisted, and, if necessary, fought. But the manner and occasion which the Government have chosen to enforce a principle sound in itself could hardly have been more unfortunate.

At the last moment the Government have invoked a principle which they had been content to overlook so long as negotiations held any promise of success. It was well known to everybody that the Trade Unions Congress had had it in mind for days, and probably for months, to act as it is acting in support of the miners if, in its view, no reasonable offer had been made to them. The Government, so far as anybody is aware, gave no warning and uttered no syllable of protest. Even after the Trade Unions Congress had formally declared its policy the Government continued to act as though no fresh question of principle had been raised. Then something happened. Either the Cabinet became suddenly convinced that the negotiations were hopeless or the wild men got control. It decided to shift the whole issue on to the constitutional question of the right of the Trade Unions Congress to call a general strike and refused to reopen negotiations unless this threat were unconditionally withdrawn. It backed this up by quoting as though it were part of the official policy – which it was not – the interference by a single union with the editorial comment of the 'Daily Mail.' To exaggerate and falsify in a document of this importance an incident for which the Congress immediately disclaimed responsibility was an indication of a want of balance which it is hard to excuse. The Government, in fact, could hardly have done more to throw doubt on the sincerity of their appeal to principle. If the principle was to be made the cardinal issue it should have been made plain beforehand. To keep it in the background until the last moment and then to use it, apparently, as merely the handiest weapon of attack was to discredit their good faith as much as their good sense.

At a certain point on Sunday night the negotiations, as explained by our London correspondent, reached something very close to agreement. Had this stage been reached even one day earlier there appears to be some reason to believe that a settlement would have been reached. But we do not know what the formula was or what alterations in it were made on Sunday. What is known is that while the miners were considering, the Government hardened. Perhaps the incident at the 'Daily Mail' offices supplied the last straw. However it came about the die-hards of the Government secured the upper hand, the ultimatum was dispatched, and the issues of peace and war were determined. Is it not possible even now to recall the precious moment at which a settlement appears to have been within sight? The Government say the notices must be withdrawn before negotiations can be resumed. The Trade Unions Congress and individual Labour leaders still assert that a settlement is possible. If they really believe that, is there any reason why they should not withdraw the strike notices on the understanding that negotiations shall be immediately resumed? In return the least the Government could do would be to secure the immediate withdrawal of the notices in the coalfields by granting the short extension of the subsidy which they previously contemplated. We should then be in the only position from which a settlement, if one is at all possible, is likely to be won. The prospect otherwise is one which nobody can contemplate without dismay. Lack of time and blunders on one side and the other have rushed matters to an extreme from which all parties, and probably not least the Trade Unions Congress, are anxious to extricate themselves by any means possible. The means are there if they will but seize them.

p.8

OUR LONDON CORRESPONDENCE
By Private Wire.

London, Monday Night.

PARLIAMENT HAS ITS CHANCE.

To-day for the first time, the House of Commons had a chance of intervening in the coal dispute, and conciliation between the two front benches went so far that one could only grieve that Parliament had not been called in before.

Mr. Baldwin spoke his piece, but one had the feeling that the militants in his Cabinet had taught it to him. His lamentation over the destruction of his policy of industrial peace and goodwill was his own. One felt that the firm insistence on the general strike notices as the *casus belli* had been imposed upon him by his own die-hards, who it is scarcely too uncharitable to suppose were not ill-pleased that the fight had come and that Mr. Baldwin had come up to the scratch.

The rest of the debate gradually developed into what amounted to a resumption of the negotiations. Mr. Lloyd George did great service by exposing the inconsistency of negotiating on Saturday after the strike notices had been issued and then making the strike notices the occasion for breaking off negotiations with startling suddenness on Sunday night, or rather Monday morning, during the absence of the Labour negotiators.

The only new fact was that one union on its own account, without consulting anybody, declared an unauthorised strike against a newspaper. It was a mere frontier incident, and when a frontier incident starts a war everyone knows that it is an excuse.

In the Lobby, after the debate had been going on for some time, the noticeable thing was a sort of incredulity and optimism. Members could not quite bring themselves to believe that with this atmosphere of conciliation inside the House nothing could be done at the last minute to avert the catastrophe. How it was to be done nobody knew but many people – I think most – clung to the hope, almost to the belief, that somehow or other it would be done.

ON THE EVE OF THE GREAT STOPPAGE.

Tomorrow Fleet Street visualises a silent place with a few busy centres – the Irish, Dominion, American and foreign newspaper offices. Great preparations are being made, especially by the Americans, to describe England for the first time in the throes of a general stoppage. The placard in the Post Office windows to-day announcing the reduction of the mails practically to letters and postcards startled even the dullest people to the possibilities before us, and the vans this morning bringing bedding into the city for banks and offices where clerks are going to sleep in until transport is normal was another excitement.

Many offices, by the way, whose business is immediately hit by the strike are starting their summer holiday arrangements, and crowds of clerks went off to-day to the Continent. Our American visitors are leaving quickly and coming Americans are changing their route.

One of the main questions people are asking is about petrol supplies. The taxicab men, who at first seemed likely to be among the few people who would benefit, are now doubtful – those who did not intend to strike – whether they will be able to get supplies. The ability of the Government to provide petrol for private motors will be one of the first tests of the strike.

GETTING READY.

The railway stations were noticeably busy during the day. Most of the long-distance trains both in and out of London were crowded, for people who must travel were going while the going was good. The afternoon Scottish express from Euston had to be duplicated. The news from the south coast resorts is that many holiday-makers have cancelled their rooms to-day by telegram or telephone.

No one knows what will be the situation to-morrow, but there is a general hope that the mobilisation of private motors and charabancs by the O.M.S. will enable people to get in and out. Round the entrances to Hyde Park there were crowds seeing what they could through the railings of the preparations for creating London's milk-distributing centre. The organisation will be much the same as in 1921. Workmen were seen putting up huts on the pitches of the orators at the Marble Arch for use by the administrative staff and as canteens for the lorry-drivers.

The Transport Ministry has a list of many thousand car owners who are ready to surrender their motors for use in fetching milk from the country to the Park and thence to the shops. During the day lorries, pantechnicons, and vans were continually coming to the park, but they were all sent away until to-morrow morning.

An official stated that the service can muster nearly a quarter of a million commercial motors if necessary.

STRANGE SIGNS.

On the lunch table at one club to-day appeared a notice to members warning them that in the event of a general strike the menu would be cut down and certain foodstuffs might be limited. This was, in order of time, the first sign of emergency that confronted the ordinary man going about his day's routine.

In the city things looked much as usual, though the streets seemed unusually full and the people animated in a curiously expectant way. Something was missing in the scene – the newspaper sellers. The remaining evening paper sold very quickly – at the Bank a man was demanding and getting twopence for it, the earliest example of strike profiteering. . . .

THE AVERAGE STRIKER.

There never was a conflict into which the average combatants – for it will be impossible if this conflict continues to be completely a non-combatant – go with more distaste. Take the man's side. Correspondents in the Battersea and Clapham areas tell me that among the railwaymen and their families there is only despondency and determination, with little belief in any personal benefit in the end.

Passengers on the 'buses who ask the conductors what they will do tomorrow when they strike are told that they will get along on the union strike pay as well as they can. The newspaper sellers, who are mainly without evening papers to-day, have in most cases no strike pay. But if you ask any of them where they 'come in' you get the same reply – 'It's to help the miners.' It is impossible not to be impressed by the unselfishness behind the ordinary individual striker in this big divide.

It is also remarkable to find how general it is among the average City man to find a complete distrust in the coalowners and belief that they will never modernise their business unless the Government compels them to do so, and an idea that they have done less than other employers for their business on the theory that they will in the end be bought out. This is felt even by those who are in their thousands ready to take their part to fight the strike, which they believe is a direct attack on the State.

The ill-advised attack by a section of the workers against certain London newspapers has greatly increased this belief that the existence even of a free press is threatened.

CROWD OF 5,000 IN PARLIAMENT SQUARE.

There were scenes reminiscent of 1914 around the House of Parliament last night. The crowd lined both sides of Bridge Street, and in Parliament Square at one time there was a crowd estimated at 5,000. The people waited silently watching the comings and goings of members of Parliament.

Downing Street was impassable throughout the evening, and there were dozens of extra police on duty.

The crowd outside the Houses of Parliament grew during the evening until on the rising of the House at a quarter past eleven it completely blocked Parliament Square. It was only with difficulty and with the aid of many scores of police that a way was cleared for the cars and taxis leaving Palace Yard. A section of the crowd amused itself for three-quarters of an hour by singing 'The Red Flag' and raising cheers for the miners. At one time another section of the crowd began to sing 'God Save the King' and there was a rush in the direction of the singers. The police, however, were able to keep the crowd in check and there was no disorder.

Leader   ## INDUSTRIAL WAR PSYCHOLOGY.

'It is war,' the Labour members are reported to have said as they reassembled in the House yesterday, and the remark would be echoed by thousands of parlour Mussolinis and little Lenins as they gloated over the reports in the evening papers. For some people, unfortunately, like war, and the evening papers were full of the forms and phrases of a state of war. The call for volunteers, the appeals (from both sides) for unquestioning loyalty, the absolute conviction (on both sides) of the irrational but nevertheless culpable wickedness of the other side, the suppression of newspapers, prolonged negotiations ending in ultimatum and breakdown, the demand for surrender as a preliminary to renewed negotiations, the emergence of war controls, price-fixing, and the whole machinery of absolutism in government suggested 1914 or 1918 rather than 1926. Some people like the excitement of it all; they see themselves in command, giving rapid decisions that determine the destiny of nations (or at any rate unions), making history, or at any rate securing publicity. The familiar phenomenon recurs of Government supporters emerging from their customary, and probably deserved, obscurity to direct 'controls' as Commissioners, and strong, silent businessmen sacrificing their

39

leisure to serve on committees that sometimes lead to knighthoods. It is all very exhilarating – to those who like it. At the same time it is very dangerous. It excites a temper that makes compromise difficult, a temper in which people become 'bitter-enders' against their better judgment. And it is uncalled for; because a strike, even a general strike, is not war.

The essence of a strike, or a lock-out, is not violence or force, but passive resistance. The parties to the dispute do not attack each other (in this country; in America and South Africa they do occasionally use guns) except in words; they agree to do nothing, and to see which can hold out longest. It is a painful and an irrational proceeding; but no one has been able to find a substitute, and it is not confined to disputes over the price of labour. Strikes occur – though they are not called strikes – over other prices. Only last week the American section of the spinning industry, dissatisfied with the prices they were receiving, decided to close down for a week: a strike against the yarn buyer. In 1920, just before prices broke, the stores could not sell their stocks; the consumers had 'locked them out.' The price of labour has immediate human consequences that put it in a category by itself among prices. But it remains a price, and until society can come to some agreed principles as to what constitutes a Just Price disputes will continue to arise, and to be settled by the refusal to buy or sell. Society suffers inconvenience because it is held together by buying and selling but terminology and still more the psychology, of war is out of place. Industrial disputes are not war, but business.

p.9

ARMY AND THE CRISIS.
Some Wild Rumours in Circulation.

(From our London Staff.)

Fleet Street, Monday.

The War Office announced this morning that there is no objection to officers on the Reserve of Officers offering themselves to local organisations for the maintenance of order and vital services. There was an immediate response to this, and during the day officers on the Reserve have been pouring into the War Office. Indeed, a very large proportion of the officers available have already volunteered.

All leave has been stopped in the army, but the statement made earlier in the day in a newspaper that all regiments are standing ready to move is quite untrue. It probably arose from a report that some detachments are to be moved from the South of

England to the camp at Catterick in Yorkshire. The Government official who is charged with the duty of keeping the press informed about the arrangements for the strike mentioned to-night that what he called 'a malicious rumour' is going about to the effect that the death penalty in the army has been reimposed, and that 'many hundreds of men have already been shot.' It is true, of course, that the death penalty for disobedience of orders on active service was reimposed as part of the Army (Annual) Act recently. It appears in the Army (Annual) Act every year, and the passage of the Act is a regular feature of every new session.

At present, needless to say, the soldiers are not on active service. The rumour about soldiers having been shot was quoted as an example of the wild rumours that are in circulation, but the official was not able to disclose the place of origin of the story.

p.17

CORRESPONDENCE

PROTECTION FOR NON-STRIKERS?

To the Editor of the Manchester Guardian.

Sir,–The manifesto of the Trade Unions Congress declaring a general strike will of necessity spread great consternation amongst many of the workers in the various trades now involved in the dispute. It is common knowledge that great numbers of working men are bitterly opposed to strikes, realising their ineffectiveness and the great hardships and privations which follow. The tyranny of the trade union is so great that members must obey its mandates and come out, breaking off contracts of service which may exist between employers and employees, the trade unions, of course, always arranging, when the dispute is ended, that the employee shall return to work without victimisation by the employer.

May I here suggest that, inasmuch as a general strike is now declared to be a direct challenge to his Majesty's Government, the Premier shall immediately give an assurance to all workers who decide to remain at work during the crisis, that a settlement of the dispute shall include the guarantee of protection against victimisation by the trade unions? This will ensure for the worker full liberty to decide for himself without fear or favour.–Yours, &c.,

May 3. HUGH HOWARTH.

WORK OF THE CIVIL COMMISSIONER.
A Perfectly Organised Machine Ready.

TRANSPORT PLANS

(From our Special Correspondent.)

Liverpool, Monday.

If the hours which have separated the threat of a general strike from the execution of that threat had been weeks, there could hardly have been assembled a more perfectly organised machine than the one of which I have been permitted a glimpse at the offices here of the Civil Commissioner of the North-western area. In each of many rooms in a building guarded by police officers is a map of the British Isles with the area under the control of the Commissioner (extending from Cumberland to Merionethshire) minutely divided into sub-districts. There are comprehensive lists of traders and all those concerned in the provision of essential supplies; and in the hands of the Road Commissioner is the name of the owner of every vehicle which could possibly be used for road transport. This afternoon a workman was busy fixing additional telephone communication – the last touch which completed the organisation.

There prevailed everywhere the greatest confidence in the efficiency of the machine. 'Almost normal services' was the phrase used by Major G. Hennessy, M.P., the Civil Commissioner, and almost everyone to whom I spoke. Food and fuel distribution, transport, the postal services, and municipal undertakings such as gas, water, and electricity, are the 'essential services,' which every endeavour will be made to maintain. The latter will be left as far as possible to the measures independently taken by local authorities.

Not Strike-Breaking
Under the state of emergency Major Hennessy is empowered (as it was expressed to me) 'practically as necessity demands.' He is especially anxious to emphasise that his system is in no sense a strike-breaking organisation, and that he is enrolling volunteers only for the above-mentioned essential services. His central divisional staff will be available to assist where required, the local committees in the area. In an appeal issued yesterday Major Hennessy says:—

The sands have run out, and in the grave emergency which has arisen the Government, acting on behalf of the whole nation, must ensure that those services which are essential to the national wellbeing continue in operation. I therefore appeal with every confidence to all citizens to do their utmost to support the authority of the King's Government.

This can best be done by offering their services at the local recruiting station, by refraining from hasty judgment or action, and by doing everything in their power to promote goodwill and a just settlement of the present trouble.

Road Transport Plans.

Colonel Tudsbury, Road Commissioner for the area, said that he had 'a very complete transport organisation,' and in addition to this his department have to-day been offered the loan of thousands of vehicles, from motor-lorries and steam waggons to motorcycle combinations. 'The organisation is simply and solely to assist the distribution of foodstuffs and fuel,' he added. 'It has no connection at all with any volunteer organisation such as the O.M.S. We hope that even trade unionists will continue to work where they are employed in the distribution of foodstuffs, and if any additional assistance is required members of the community will do their bit.'

Here, as in other sections of the organisation, the Government system will operate only where the need arises. In the majority of cases, Colonel Tudsbury anticipated, private firms and traders would find their own transport arrangements sufficient and would carry on as usual, without interference from the Government. Passenger services are being left to individual firms, which may make private arrangements for bringing their employees to work, and to owners of motor-coaches, who are expected to institute services on paying routes.

The Food Supplies.

In charge of the food supply in the area is Sir Arnold Rushton, a former Lord Mayor of Liverpool, who also made it clear that his organisation was designed not to interfere with the normal course of things, but only to help the traders in circumstances under which any of them might not be able to help themselves.

'We are confident,' he said, 'that we shall keep up a fairly normal food supply, though the public must be warned that there will have to be economy in consumption. We have been inundated with offers of assistance from trade associations of all kinds, and individual traders themselves are doing all that is possible to make our work easy.'

So far as Liverpool itself is concerned, sufficient stocks of coal are in hand to continue the normal working of the gas and electricity departments for a considerable time. The normal consumption of the electricity plant is 4,000 tons a week, and 30,000 tons are said to be in stock. An official of the gas department reported that there was sufficient coal to last 'for months.'

A special meeting of coal merchants yesterday was addressed by Councillor G.Y. Williamson, emergency coal officer for the area, who said that the rationing order (under which not more than one hundred-weight weekly is to be supplied to any one householder, and then only when his stock is below five cwt.) would be fully carried out. Merchants are to make a declaration of the stocks of coal they have at present in hand.

p.11

STRIKE POSITION IN MANCHESTER.
T.U.C. Instructions to be Observed.

GAS AND ELECTRICITY.
Position Obscure: Full Supply Hoped For.

As far as we were able to ascertain yeterday, the instructions of the General Council of the Trade Unions Congress are being acted upon by the various bodies of workers affected by them in the Manchester area. Railway workers, tramwaymen, carters, dockers, power enginemen and firemen, printers, iron and steel workers, vehicle builders and builders on work other than houses and hospitals all announced their intention to cease work at midnight or at the close of their night labours.

Last night the position with regard to the production of gas and electricity in the city, was rather obscure. The officials declared that there was no fear of the supplies running short for the time being, and said that a full supply will be maintained as long as possible. Beyond that little can be said at present. The recommendation of the T.U.C. was to the effect that the trade unions connected with these public supplies 'should co-operate with the object of ceasing to supply power,' and it added a request that the executives of these unions should meet at once 'with a view to formulating common policy.'

After a meeting early in the day the Electrical Trades Union, which has its headquarters in Manchester, issued an instruction to its branches to take 'joint action along with any other section of men who have ceased work on transport, printing, engineering, and steel production.' How this will work out remains to be seen. At the best it seems rather indefinite.

A Taxi-Cab Service.

One of the difficulties which most business people will experience at once will be that of getting to and from business with no trains or trams running – though Mr. Mattinson, general manager of the Manchester tramways, announces that strenuous

44

efforts will be made to maintain 'as good a service as possible.' The taxi owner-drivers and some charabanc owners have stepped into the breach with promises to start services on something like a score of routes into and out of the centre of the city at cheap rates, and are hoping to maintain these services from half-past seven in the morning until midnight. The taxicab routes are confined to a radius of about two and a half miles from Albert Square, and each cab will take five passengers at the fare of sixpence a passenger. The charabancs are expected to cover longer distances.

It is impossible at the moment to indicate how many workers will be immediately thrown out of work in the Manchester district by the strike, but the number will be very large. The railwaymen alone number about 30,000, the members of the Dock, Wharf, Riverside, and General Workers' Union another 30,000, and the transport members of the National Union of Distributive Workers about 15,000; all of these may not be affected, as official orders have been given not to bring out 'safety' men.

Strike Committee.

Last night Councillor W. Mellor, who, as secretary of the Trades and Labour Council, is one of the local representatives of the T.U.C., gave the assurance that every effort will be made to co-operate with local authorities in ensuring the safety of the food supplies of the two cities and district and 'other essential services.' The conduct of the strike operations here has now been taken over by a central committee, which was formed at a meeting of representatives of trade unions in Salford yesterday afternoon. This committee is to act for the North-western area in general, which includes Lancashire, Cheshire, Westmorland, Cumberland, North Wales, and part of North Derbyshire. A sub-committee of this body is to wait upon Sir Robert Peacock, the Chief Constable of Manchester, this morning to discuss the subject of the supplies of milk and other food.

p.11

SPECIAL POLICE.

As announced in the 'Manchester Guardian' yesterday, an inspection of the Manchester special police will take place this morning. In an interview yesterday the Chief Constable (Sir Robert Peacock) explained that a force of special constables was formed in Manchester during the war and that the purpose of to-day's inspection was to discover the present strength of this force.

Sir Robert added that volunteers were now being enrolled as special constables, and he pointed out that any persons desirous of volunteering for that force could do so on application to the training school attached to the London Road fire station. But it must be distinctly understood, he said, that the force was simply for the maintenance of law and order and had no connection whatever with O.M.S. or any scheme of road transport or food supplies.

SALFORD SPECIALS

The Chief Constable of Salford (Major Godfrey) yesterday sent out a circular letter to a number of men who served as special constables during the last labour trouble in the city asking if they are willing to enrol again.

p.9

START OF STRIKE IN MANCHESTER.
Midnight Expresses Leave.

WILL THEY REACH LONDON?
Stations Picketed.

The three midnight trains to London (Euston and St. Pancras) left the London Road, Victoria, and Central stations, Manchester, without incident. There were hardly a score of passengers on the London Road train, which is usually crowded, and the luggage vans were almost empty. According to railway employees this was the last train that would leave the station.

The driver told a 'Manchester Guardian' representative that he would take the train as far as Rugby, where he was customarily relieved by another driver; whether this driver would report for duty he was unable to say. In the event of signalmen leaving work before six o'clock the train would, of course, be unable to reach Euston.

A few minutes after midnight four pickets took up positions at the bottom of the drive leading to London Road Station, and it was stated that similar measures were being taken at all Manchester stations.

Question of 'Skeleton' Service.

Inquiries at the Central and Victoria Stations, Manchester, early this morning revealed the fact that the railway authorities were quite in the dark as to the possibility of restricted services to-day. At both stations the night staff was on duty and continued on duty until 6 a.m. It remained to be seen how many men put in an appearance at that hour before it could be decided what, if any, make-shift service could be devised.

The midnight train to St. Pancras carried only a small contingent of passengers and it was uncertain whether the train could get beyond Derby. The scene at the station was one of order, though groups of men were gathered at the entrance. The 11 50 p.m. train from Liverpool arrived as usual and discharged a moderate number of passengers. It was expected that the parcel train, due to arrive at 3 2 a.m. and the newspaper train, due in Manchester at 5 15 a.m., both from London, would arrive as usual, but there was uncertainty as to the arrival of the 6 48 a.m. train.

Explaining the difficulty in arranging a 'skeleton' service a railway official observed: 'We shall have to be guided by circumstances. If the signalmen come out we shall be "scotched." ' At all stations the question of the extent of the loyalty of the men to the call of the General Council of the Trades Union Congress was the factor which made it difficult to prophecy how far it will be possible to run some sort of service to-day.

At Victoria Station an official said: 'If we get the men to work the trains we shall work them. We shall have to wait until six o'clock before we know what trains we shall be able to work.' During yesterday and last night a number of goods trains due out of Victoria were cancelled.

TRAMWAYMEN'S DECISION.

A mass meeting of the Manchester tramwaymen was held at midnight in the Co-operative Hall, Downing Street, to decide on the men's action in the dispute. The men were solidly in favour of coming out as from midnight.

Over 5,000 men assembled, and hundreds were unable to gain admission. The large hall was crowded and an overflow meeting in the Assembly Hall was similarly filled.

It was announced during the meeting that the Salford Corporation had last night posted notices to the effect that any man in the employment of the tramways undertaking failing to report himself for duty this morning will be dismissed, and that men must return their uniforms within twenty-four hours.

Power for electrical transport service in Manchester was cut off at 2 a.m. to-day, and it was stated early this morning that if attempts were made to run the tramway service by voluntary labour the labour for electrical lighting would also be withdrawn.

It was not possible to obtain confirmation of the reported Salford threat to tramway workers.

GERMAN LABOUR AND THE CRISIS.
Question of Support.

(From our own Correspondent.)

Berlin, Monday.

Events in England are being followed with the greatest interest here. This evening's papers devote columns to the crisis. Even papers usually hostile to Labour comment on the backward organisation and structure of the British mining industry. The German Labour press represent the conflict as one between retrograde mineowners and progressive miners, while papers of the extreme Left naturally pretend that the British unions have revolutionary aims.

German trade unions are, of course, entirely sympathetic with the British, although they anticipate coming events with great concern, for no one knows as well as German labour knows from personal experience what a fearful calamity a general strike must be.

The German Miners' Union has issued a declaration of solidarity with the British miners, but whether the German unions will be able to offer any effective help is very doubtful. There is no immediate prospect of German coal being exported to England. Should the British mining strike be prolonged, as it was in 1921, and should the German coal industry attempt to replete dwindling British reserves, the attempt will certainly be resisted by German miners. But that is a remote contingency, although if it were to come about then the British strike must extend to Germany.

On the markets where there is competition between German and British coal (Hamburg, for example), the German coal industry may profit momentarily. It is not likely that the German miners will interfere with the despatch of German coal to these markets. Interference of such kind would indeed be futile, and would be of hardly any benefit to the British miners.

The German unions may decide to help the British unions financially, just as they did the Danish unions in the dockyard strike a few months ago. But no sum the German unions could afford would be big enough to make an appreciable difference. Generally speaking the German unions will do all they can and will use all their influence with the international labour organisations, although their help will not be able to affect the decision in England, at least not in the material sense.

U.S. PRESS COMMENT.

Labour Leaders' 'Instinct for Jugular Vein.'

(Reuter's Telegram.)

New York, Monday.

The 'New York Times' leader this morning, while expressing confidence in the ability of the British people to meet courageously the formidable menace of a general strike, severely condemns the tactics of British Labour. Referring to the fact that the Labour leaders have made concessions only in matters of health and food supplies, the paper suggests:–

'If it is to be war which they are to conduct they may as well make it consistently ruthless. Starvation by a complete blockade would be a powerful weapon in their hands. The Labour leaders seek to show they have "an instinct for the jugular vein." On such terms no Government could surrender and preserve not merely the self-respect but its life.'

SUSPENSION OF PUBLICATION.

We regret to state that in consequence of the strike of certain unions connected with the printing trade it is probable that the 'Manchester Guardian' will be compelled to suspend publication to-day until further notice. In that case a small typescript sheet of news and comment will be sent free to postal subscribers and on prepayment of postage to any other of our readers who may send a request to the Manager to that effect. Copies may also be obtained at the 'Guardian' Office.

The workforce of the Manchester Guardian actually appealed to the General Council of the TUC for permission to be exempt from the strike. Their plea, however, alongside others registered by papers such as the 'Daily Herald' sympathetic to the labour movement, was turned down.

THE TRADE UNIONS CONGRESS AND THE PRESS.

The decision of the Trade Unions Congress to call out the printers and to silence the press seems to us a singularly misguided policy, and we cannot believe it will be maintained. To put the press out of action gives a most dangerous power to the Government, which, by its control of broadcasting, will enjoy a complete monopoly in the distribution of news and views. Is this desired by the Trade Unions Congress and the miners? In a time of crisis a free press is specially needed, because it is important to keep open every channel through which moderate opinion can express itself. It is no advantage to the nation and it is certainly no advantage to the workers that the issues should be left to the brutal decision of force and that reason and argument should have no influence on conduct. Yet this is what will happen if the newspapers do not appear. There will be no opportunity for discussion, and consequently the moderate forces, which might hope to influence the Government and public opinion, will count for very little. And if this controversy is not settled by moderate opinion it will be settled by the die-hards, and such a settlement will be a catastrophe.

STOP-PRESS NEWS.

THE STRIKE'S BEGINNING.

The general strike of workers engaged in transport and other industries came into effect at midnight. At 1 a.m. the London General Omnibus Company reported everything proceeding in orderly fashion and omnibuses were being run to their various garages and night services concluded. Underground trains were also taken to their proper depots.

At Euston men worked out their turns, but none booked on after midnight. Trains left Paddington according to the timetable up to 12 30, at which hour the last train in the night service left.

The train scheduled to reach Euston from the North at 5 a.m. was expected in London to complete its journey, as was the 11 50 from Euston to the North.

T.U.C. APPEAL AGAINST DISORDER.

The General Council of the Trade Unions Congress last night issued a final message of appeal to workers to follow the instructions issued, according to the 'Daily Herald,' by union leaders: – 'Let none be disturbed by rumours or driven to panic to betray the cause. Violence and disorder must be everywhere avoided no matter what the incitement. Stand firm and we shall win.' The appeal opens with the statement that the trade unions have not entered on the struggle without counting the cost and are fighting to maintain the standard of living.

M. Oudegeest, secretary of the International Federation of Trade Unions, stated yesterday (says an Exchange Amsterdam telegram) that the Federation embracing the trade unions of 23 countries and disposing in cash 200 million Dutch guilders, would strongly support the British Trade Unions Congress. The British Trade Unions Congress, he added, might hold out in the struggle for four or five weeks without financial support from the Continent, 'and,' declared M. Oudegeest, 'I do not believe that the strike will last longer.'

As predicted, the 'Guardian' on Wednesday May 5 was restricted to two sides of typescript.

MANCHESTER GUARDIAN BULLETIN

Wednesday May 5 1926

Leader   **IN THE DARK**

It is a singular commentary on the biggest industrial upheaval of our time that the public has not been told what was the formula upon which peace was all but built on Sunday night. For some reason or other an offer made by Mr. Baldwin, which is understood to have encouraged high hopes of a settlement amongst the trade union leaders, was abandoned by its author (presumably on the decision of a cabinet meeting which had been held in the meantime) without waiting for the final decision of the Trade Unions Congress upon it. In its place an ultimatum was substituted, demanding the unconditional withdrawal of the general strike notices as a condition of further negotiations. The subsidy, the nine months' inquiry, the six weeks' negotiations on the report have gone for nothing and we are plunged into a national strike without being told the essential elements of the final dividing issues.

We must suppose that in the Government's view all that now matters is the constitutional question raised by the general strike and that this must be settled before we can get back to any kind of discussion of the coal problem. That, in fact, is the plain meaning of the ultimatum but in this matter also we are left in ignorance of the most vital facts. We know, in this case, the Government's terms – unconditional withdrawal of the strike notices. But we do not know the terms of the Trade Unions Congress. What are their conditions? What are they fighting for? Beyond the fact that they are fighting for what they regard as a decent standard of living for the miners we doubt if they know themselves. Certainly they have never told the public. No trade union leader has ever attempted to define the standard of living which would be acceptable below the present standard. The present standard the Trade Unions Congress has formally declared to be unobtainable under present circumstances. What then are they fighting for? Are they fighting for the moon or for something attainable? If it is attainable why do they not say what it is?

PARLIAMENT – The budget resolutions were passed and Commons adjourned at 5.10 p.m. The Labour party declined, owing to the strike, to debate the betting tax, which was carried by 282 to 122. Emergency Powers Bill will be debated today. In the Lords – Lord Haldane praised Premier as mediator, but blamed Government for not continuing negotiations and urged a settlement. Lord Oxford said no Government could have refrained from taking up the challenge.

GOVERNMENT AND THE UNIONS – Our Political correspondent telegraphs:– Opinion in the lobbies yesterday was still very largely optimistic as to settlement before very long, but the more critical minded members did not share this view. They judged, I think rightly, that the thing having begun the Government will not care to negotiate until they are approached by the trade unions, and that they will not be overready or overeasy about resuming negotiations even then. It is not suggested that they will insist on 'a fight to a finish' but rather will they hold on until victory is visibly approaching. The Parliamentary Labour Party held two meetings, but no report has been made public. When Commons rose a meeting of the Conservative party was held at which Premier and other ministers were present. No report issued.

AT STRIKE HEADQUARTERS – Our Labour correspondent tele-graphs:– There are no developments to report on the side of the unions. Meetings were held yesterday at Ecclestone Square and the House of Commons of members of the General Council and the Miners' Executive. Committees have been formed to take charge of various branches of the strike. The International Miners' Federation will meet in a few days. The German miners decided yesterday to restrict overtime and output and to work in close co-operation with the transport workers, who have placed an embargo on exports to Britain. Exports to neutral markets will not be directly interfered with.

GOVERNMENT DAILY AND EVENING – The Government daily broadsheet is to be printed and published at the "Morning Post" office which has been taken over for the purpose. Editor not yet selected; representative of the government will be Mr. Caird, press secretary of the Colonial Office and the War Office. First issue promised for 9 last night.

LONDON'S CONGESTED STREETS – Our London correspondent telegraphs:– The extraordinary effect of the traffic stoppage has been that so many motor cars are being used that the traffic in London streets has almost stopped itself. Traffic was moving three abreast. No difficulty yet about petrol and tyres. Speculators bought up supplies of morning papers and rushed them on the streets in the afternoon selling for threepence and sixpence as just published. No Government motor wagons for passengers have yet appeared. There were threats at night of electricians striking. There has been no run on shops.

NEW POWERS OF SEARCH – Under the Emergency Power Act the Government have taken wide powers for police search under order of a Secretary of State of premises suspected of use in connection with any documents likely to cause sedition or hinder public safety and essential supply services.

THE STRIKE IN MANCHESTER – In Manchester yesterday no trams ran and the only trains were one from London Road to London, with a return train, and one each way between Central Station and Derby. No Local Service was attempted. Virtually all the signalmen were out, and fewer engine drivers reported for duty than in any other strike. To-day's time-table: Manchester (London Road) 9-30 a.m. via Sheffield and Nottingham, to London Marylebone (arr. 5-55 p.m.) stopping all stations. On the main roads from outer suburbs to centre of the city there was enormous motor traffic all day. Charabancs at 6d per passenger, and the 6d taxis in the inner circle, did a prosperous trade. The docks were at a standstill, but from railway sidings and markets the transport of food and other esentials continued. Early in the morning some pickets prevented provisions being moved, but the Chief Constable met a central strike committee deputation and an agreement was reached which will ensure co-operation. Gas and electricity supplies are still normal and it is hoped to maintain the output. By early afternoon 12,000 volunteers were enrolled at the Free Trade Hall alone, for various services. They included one local aviator, with aeroplane complete.

MR SAKLATVALA – Mr. Saklatvala, M.P. was brought before Sir. C. Biron at Bow Street yesterday to show cause why he should not find a surety for his good behaviour. Proceedings rose out of a speech on May Day. Defendant undertook not to speak outside the House and case was adjourned until Thursday. Bail in two sureties of £100 each.

STRIKE ITEMS – Tram service was restored at Portsmouth by sections of the men after a threat of volunteer working; skeleton service also running at Southampton, Lincoln, Leeds and Edinburgh. G.W.R. trains were run yesterday between Bala, Corwen and Ruabon by two railway firemen. The strikers did not interfere. Dutch exporters of vegetables, meats and dairy produce have suspended shipments from Rotterdam to England. The last boat from Hook of Holland to Harwich left last night.

OFFICIAL STATEMENT BY THE TUC – Last night Mr. Poulton, Chairman of the T.U.C. Publicity Committee said; 'Reports we have received from all over the Country from Land's End to John O'Groats have surpassed all expectations. The General Council's difficulty has been to keep men at work in the trades that are in the second line of defence. All the reports indicate that the strike is being conducted in an orderly and good-tempered manner. The arrangements in regard to food transport, etc., are working quite satisfactorily in accordance with the instructions issued. So far as we can judge from the information at our disposal there is whole hearted support of the policy agreed upon at the conference of the Trade Union Executive in London last week'. A Government spokesman last night stated – 'This is the completest strike we have ever had especially on the railways'.

A GLASGOW INCIDENT – Our special correspondent at Glasgow telegraphs that hooligans in Parkhead and Shettleton district stopped two motor 'buses going to mining village of Hamilton, compelled the passengers to dismount and overturned the 'buses in the roadway. No one was injured. Mounted police were called out to patrol the district. It is reported that one or two private service motor 'buses have been pelted with stones by irresponsible demonstrators not directly concerned with the strike.

TENNIS AND CRICKET – Inter-club tennis championship: L. Lees and Mr. Woosman (Manchester 11) beat E.M. Baerlein and W. Renshaw (Manchester 1), 6-2, 6-2, 6-2. Australians 333 (Gregory 120 not out); Leicester 96 (Macartney 5 for 9) and 15 for 1. Drawn. Lancashire 179 and 180 for 6; Warwick 140 and 91 for 3. Drawn. Surrey 243 and 145 for 3; Hampshire 182 and 118 for 4. Drawn. Northamption 111 and 227; Notts 180 and 160 for 6. Notts won by 4 wickets. Cambridge University 89; Middlesex 223. Abandoned.

Yorkshire 359 and 6 for none; Essex 110 and 254. Yorkshire won by 10 wickets.

It is interesting that, despite the restrictions on news space, the 'Guardian' always took the opportunity to give details of the major sporting events.

PARIS OPINION – Our Paris correspondent telegraphs – 'French opinion is amazed at the seeming meaninglessness of the social collision, unprecedented in history yet totally unrevolutionary which is occurring among politically the quietest people in the world. Bad management on the part of the leaders of the Nation on both sides is said to be the cause. The moral is drawn in favour of inflation. England, it is said, is paying for the worship of the gold standard.'

On Thursday May 6 the Guardian appeared in something resembling its usual format but restricted to a single page priced at one penny.

Thursday May 6 1926

Leader   **EMERGENCY REGULATIONS.**

The first day of the strike passed off, in a sense, uneventfully. The absence of trains and trams is not a new thing; it was borne good humouredly, and in no part of the country did any kind of serious disturbance occur. Already, by the second day, there have been ominous signs that this peaceful state of affairs is gradually giving way to a more dangerous temper. From various parts of the country incidents are reported which involved minor damage to property, and in some cases in personal injuries. Nothing that has happened so far is of serious consequence in itself, but it is plain enough that every day the strike lasts the strain on the nerves will be greater, the number of incidents will grow and the danger to life and property become more serious. It is true that on the other hand the capacity of the nation, after the first shock, to adjust itself to the complete disarrangement of its ordinary methods of living and working is already beginning to assert itself, and that transport facilities, in particular, are likely to improve with time. But this does not alter the fact that on the whole the situation must grow from bad to worse, partly through the cumulative effects of the slowing down of industry, but even more through the cumulative effects of nerve strain. This remains true, even though there is evidence of some dissatisfaction among the members of certain unions with the way in which, without consultation, their executives have put them under the absolute orders of the Trade Unions Congress. If, here and there, resentment should lead to a breakaway from the official policy the general temper of the trade unions appears to be hardening, like that of the Government, and defections from the general strike orders, if they occur, may be balanced by fresh recruits in other industries.

Is this to be a struggle of exhaustion, like that of the great war? If so the symptoms of disorder which have already been noted can only lead in the end to rioting and bloodshed. A struggle of exhaustion on this scale can rarely end without scenes of violence on a scale of which for generations this country has had no experience. It is perfectly true, as the Home Secretary said yesterday, that once a conflict of this kind has broken out the Government must use all its powers to maintain the major public services. The technical branches of the army and navy are available for supplying certain services who have been or may be withdrawn and cannnot easily be replaced. There is no reason why, if necessary, they should not be used. Sir William Joynson-Hicks has taken steps to use them for the supply of electricity and motor spirit and for railway transport. But some other regulations which he has introduced under the Emergency Powers Act are highly dangerous. The right of arrest without warrant is, in particular, one which, even in hands more cautious than those of the present Home Secretary, is far more likely to be abused than to serve the cause of order and justice. It is typical of the kind of power which should not be exercised, save in the most extreme circumstances. That the Government should prepare for the worst is not objectionable, but to assume the worst before it has happened is provocative.

HOUSE OF COMMONS.

WHY THE NEGOTIATIONS BROKE DOWN.

Important Statement by Party Leaders.

In the House of Commons yesterday, the Home Secretary moved the confirmation of the regulations under the Emergency Powers Act. He said the regulations were for one month only, after which their renewal must be the subject of and proclamation and order of the House. The Government and the whole country hoped it would not be necessary to extend the period. Explaining the purport and the regulations, he pointed out that they would enable the Government to take possession of lands, buildings and various undertakings, such as electricity and gas, so that if necessary they could be kept in operation for the benefit of the nation as a whole.

Mr. T.P. O'Connor asked why did not the parties come together again. What was the dignity of any man, compared with this great disaster?

Mr. Clynes said that in the end Labour could not be beaten.

Lord Hugh Cecil, while urging that the first step towards a solution of the difficulty was that the general strike should come to an end, said don't let us speak about having victory over one another. Let us try by commonsense to get the best settlement we can.

Mr. J.H. Thomas said that the speech of Lord Hugh Cecil, delivered from a detached point of view, was the one contribution which had been made to the problem this afternoon.

'Let there be no misunderstanding,' said Mr. Thomas. 'There was no formula. At eleven o'clock on Sunday night I had not a formula, but the Prime Minister's own words in his own handwriting in my possession as a means of settling, and I accepted it on behalf of the T.U.C. We had not only accepted it, but had taken the responsibility of saying: "Never mind what the miners or anybody else say, we accept it." ' These were words, explained Mr. Thomas that the Prime Minister himself had written down as being a common basis of settlement.

The Prime Minister said he did not think his recollection was very different from what had been said. The discussion that was being held was very private, and what his colleagues, Lord Birkenhead and the Minister of Labour and himself, were endeavouring to do on their side was to get an assurance from the trades council that they felt confident that a settlement would be arrived at on the lines of the report. What he was clear about was that they were going to see the miners' executive, which had been summoned from the country, on the subject to see if they could get some such assurance from them.

They went to see the miners about 11 o'clock and he (the Prime Minister) was in a position of great anxiety of negotiating under a threat. He doubted the wisdom of it, but he ran the risk of the situation. It was whilst the Trades Unions Council were asking the miners, and whilst he and his colleagues were explaining to the Council the significance of it, that they learned of the first active move and that a general strike was actually being made. They heard by telephone that they were trying to in those circles to suppress the press. They felt that in those circumstances the whole situation was completely changed.

The Prime Minister said the Government felt that this was more than a threat. This was direct action of the worst kind. Under these circumstances the Government had to take its stand. He confirmed what he had previously said, that there was every hope of an agreement being reached if the discussions had been continued had it not been for the declaration of a general strike.

Mr. Ramsay Macdonald said that the Prime Minister knew what the mind of the representatives of the General Council was. He also knew that at that moment the General Council, having specially summoned the miners' executive, were in consultation with them in the room next door to that in which the Cabinet was sitting. Then the news about the *Daily Mail* arrived. There was never a question put by the Cabinet to the people in the other room. They were neither asked whether they knew anything about it or whether they were responsible for it or what action it was proposed to make in reference to the matter. At that time they were busy working out a formula, and the letter was received which changed the whole situation.

On the receipt of this letter, said Mr. Macdonald, his colleagues decided to send a deputation to the next room where the Government representatives were sitting, and to ask what it was all about and to explain the whole situation to them.

When the deputation arrived at that room they found the door locked and the whole place in darkness. (Labour cries of 'Shame').

THE REGULATIONS.

Earlier in the Debate

In introducing regulations under the Emergency Powers Act, the Home Secretary, referring specifically to what he described as the more unpleasant of the regulations, said that authority was given for taking possession of land, buildings, and works, and also of food and fuel and other articles essential to the life of the community. Offences in the form of acts inciting to mutiny and sedition could be dealt with summarily. Another regulation gave the right of arrest without warrant. A regulation giving a great power to the Secretary of State was the one dealing with newspapers. Under this the police might enter into any building which was suspected of being used for printing or publishing any document likely to cause mutiny or sedition.

There was a further power to call upon the forces of the Crown to assist in carrying on any service of vital importance.

Under this regulation, continued the Home Secretary, he had already made four orders. He had directed that the supply of electricity, the maintenance of electrical and mechanical machinery in the Port of London, the transport of motor spirit and the continuance of the railway services were each a vital necessity.

It was possible for the Government to take steps without telling the House of Commons, but he proposed to keep the House informed from day to day of what he was doing. He proposed that night to ask the community as a whole to enrol in much larger numbers as special constables.

The House rose at 11-45.

In the House of Lords yesterday, Lord Birkenhead said the Government were not and would not be prepared to negotiate as long as the threat to constitutional government held the field.

LABOUR'S STRIKE BULLETIN.

The publication of the T.U.C.'s strike bulletin, the 'British Worker', was held up last night while the police examined the first copy. It was afterwards issued.

STRIKE CONDITIONS.
Serious Extension Under Consideration.

(From our Labour Correspondent.

London, Wednesday.

The General Council reports that the strike is as solid as it was on Tuesday and has exceeded all expectations. Extension to other trades is now being considered. The position has become difficult in the electricity stations owing to the impossibility of distinguishing between power and lighting, and the introduction of naval ratings has stirred up feeling. The calling out of the power station men and the extension of the strike to general engineering shops are possible developments of the next day or two. The Council Committee reports that employers in many industries are stopping their works.

DISTURBANCES.
5,000 Strikers' Conflict with Police

Leeds, Wednesday.

Ugly scenes were witnessed in the chief thoroughfares of Leeds about noon to-day.

The trouble began when several thousand strikers attacked one of the emergency tramcars with lumps of coal taken from a passing lorry, a number of windows in the tram-car being smashed and passengers having narrow escapes.

The strikers rushed towards another tram-car a moment later, but were held back for a time by a strong body of police.

Amid loud cries of 'down with the police,' the strikers rushed on to them. The police backed to a narrower thoroughfare, where they defended themselves with their batons.

Several windows in the main part of Briggate were smashed by the strikers. A man was arrested, and the police managed to get him into a side street.

About 5,000 strong, the strikers dashed round another street, but the police, who had been reinforced, managed to keep them clear by their truncheons.

About ten minutes later the windows of two more tram-cars were smashed and several passengers were cut on the face.

Nottingham police prevented several attempts by strikers to march upon factories, and James Tighe was remanded in custody there to-day for endeavouring to incite a big crowd late on Tuesday night to rush the . . . .

Prisoner was stated to have delivered violent speeches while brandishing a heavy piece of iron. In arresting him the police were stoned.

Good order prevails generally in Nottinghamshire mining districts.

'THE BRITISH GAZETTE.'
Statement in Parliament.

In the House of Commons Commander Kenworthy asked the Home Secretary whether a Government newspaper known as 'The British Gazette' (loud Ministerial cheers) was being published, and whether he took full responsibility for the statements contained therein and whether the cost would come on the Home Office vote.

The Home Secretary replied: 'The answer to the first part is in the affirmative. The Government take full responsibility for matter contained in the paper, and as it is being published by Stationery Office, the cost of the publication will be borne on the Treasury vote.'

The 'British Gazette' was a particularly controversial publication being sponsored by the Government and using the premises of the 'Morning Post'. With Winston Churchill as Editor, the 'British Gazette' undertook a series of assaults on the trade union movement that prompted the TUC to set up the 'British Worker' on the premises of the Daily Herald in an attempt to redress the propaganda balance.

MEASURES AGAINST VICTIMISATION.
Notice to the Printing Trade.

OFFICIAL.

The following will appear in to-day's issue of 'The British Gazette':–

'When the present General Strike is ended, His Majesty's Government will take effectual measures to prevent the victimisation by trades unions of any man who remains at work or who may return to work, and no settlement will be agreed to by His Majesty's Government which does not provide for this for a lasting period and for its enforcement, if necessary, by penalties. No man who does his duty loyally to the country in the present crisis will be left unprotected by the State from subsequent reprisals.

FRESH NEGOTIATIONS IN VIEW.
Mr. Baldwin and Mr. Thomas.

Central News last night at 8-0 said: 'Great activity has been noticed among Labour Leaders in the last hour in the Commons. It is understood that Mr. Baldwin and Mr. Thomas are again in informal conversation with a view to seeing whether some understanding can be reached without delay. Certain conciliatory speeches delivered in the House to-night have confirmed this impression. The possibility must not be ruled out, although it is a bare one, of an early development which would be the first step to cancelling the general strike notices and recommencing negotiations.

IN MANCHESTER.

A half-hourly service was kept up on the electric line to Radcliffe. An L.N.E.A. train to London gave access in the morning to the Sheffield district and there were two trains to Derby. Some of the trains were driven by railwaymen who were working their way home, but it is hoped to keep up the same, or a better, service to-day. Road services were maintained as on Tuesday and no shortage of provisions is feared. The local authority has been instructed to enforce the order limiting household coal supplies to 1 cwt. a week. The enrolment of volunteers continued satisfactorily and the police have enlisted about 1,000 'specials.' An unsuccessful attempt was made at the Manchester City Council yesterday to criticise certain principal officials at the Town Hall 'for acting as strike-breakers in connection with transport in the city.' The chairman of the tramways committee said: 'We have had no trouble at all with our men.'

THE SALFORD TRAMWAYS.

Efforts are to be made to run a motor 'bus service in Salford as soon as possible. On Tuesday the Tramways Committee appointed a subcommittee with plenary powers, and this body yesterday decided at once to notify tramway and 'bus men that the wages due to them would be paid at the Frederick road depot during week-end, when, in accordance with their signed agreement, they must return uniforms and any other property belonging to the Corporation. It was further decided to advertise for 'bus drivers and conductors between 21 and 40 years of age to fill the vacancies.

The Salford City Council yesterday received a communication from the Mines Dept. of the Government asking them to assume local coal control.

OPINION ABROAD.

(From our own Correspondents.)

FRANCE.

Paris, Wednesday.

Newspapers devote whole pages to the English news, which swamps all other topics. Nearly all the famous political descriptive Journalists have been sent over to London, many by aeroplane. Their accounts – many columns long – are remarkable for sympathetic impartiality, this being in marked contrast to the English Language Press published here.

All French correspondents are unanimous that the movement in England is non-revolutionary, and pay tribute to the good-tempered, calm populations.

The French dockers', railwaymen's, and miners' unions have issued manifestoes in favour of the English strikers, promising assistance. At St. Quen 2,000 workers at a big automobile factory yesterday struck in sympathy. Communications with London are as follows: One train a day to Calais; one perhaps after to-night; two to Dieppe–Newhaven. The Havre–Southampton night boat runs three times a week. Aeroplane services from Paris to London greatly increased.

GERMANY.

Berlin, Wednesday.

The Miners' Union has issued a manifesto calling upon its members to prevent the export of coal to England and to refuse to work extra shifts or overtime. Definite action on the part of German unions, specially miners and transport workers, will be taken in conjunction with the International Labour organisations. Generally speaking the German trade unions are strongly in favour of showing the utmost possible solidarity with the British, although it is fully realised that little can be done here to make any material difference in England. Reports that German labour is reluctant to support British unions because the British coal industry profited by the paralysis of the German coal industry when the French occupied the Ruhr are untrue. The German coal trade does not expect to gain any lasting advantage by the strike of British Miners. German business men on the whole are more afraid of general repercussions of the strike.

JAPAN.

Kobe: Wednesday.

Delegates of the Kobe Labour Union Congress have presented to the British Consul, a manifesto making demands upon the British Government in favour of the miners and threatening, in case of non-compliance, to prevent the working of British cargoes in Japanese ports. The Consul refused to accept responsibility for its transmission. The Congress is not very influential. The demands include the abolition of the O.M.S.

ITALY.

Rome, Wednesday.

So far there have been no reactions to the British strike.

On Friday May 7 the Guardian again appeared as a one-page sheet.

Friday May 7 1926

Leader **A FIGHT TO A FINISH.**

What are we fighting about? In a sense it is as clear as daylight. The negotiations with the miners having broken down the Trade Unions Congress issued orders for a general sympathetic strike which has taken effect. The Government refuse to re-open negotiations about the mines until the general strike orders have been unconditionally withdrawn. The struggle, therefore, on this showing must go on until the T.U.C. abandons the general strike. The Government have nothing to do but ensure the preservation of law, order and, so far as it can, the essential economic services. No doubt this is the plain reading of the situation as it appears not only to the Government, but to most people who, irrespective of their opinions about the mining industry, repudiate the whole underlying theory of the general strike. That seems to us so plainly indefensible that so long as it in fact continues there seems, broadly, to be no alternative open to the Government but to act broadly as it is acting. We cannot allow the general strike to become a recognised or admissible form of government. We cannot yield to it or bargain with it. But even those who hold this view as strongly as we do ourselves must ask themselves whether the situation is so simple as the Government theory would have us believe.

The theory in fact breaks down on a strict examination of what actually happened. The mining negotiations had not been abandoned, and had not broken down when the Government declared war on the general strike and made that the supreme and, for the time being, the only issue. The mining negotiations had reached, on the contrary, a most promising stage when the Government, on its own admission abruptly ended them on the plea, which has since been shown to be without foundation that the general strike had begun. The incident at the 'Daily Mail' offices was an isolated and unauthorised anticipation of the strike, and the policy which it represents has never been sanctioned by the T.U.C. By allowing itself to be rushed by this one act of folly, the Government committed a grave mistake. It was, in fact, the Government and not the breakdown of the mining negotiations which precipitated the general strike. Even if this be admitted it may be asked how it affects the situation now that the strike is in force. It has this bearing – that it fulfils an essential condition demanded by Mr. Baldwin for the resuming of the mining negotiations – that they should be entered upon with a reasonable prospect of success. It is evident that, whatever the miners may have thought about it, the T.U.C. accepted, or had gone so near to accepting, the Government's formula that Mr. Baldwin would have felt no difficulty about continuing negotiations with it on the basis of a short extension of the subsidy and a withdrawal of the coalowners' notices. The only thing which prevented these continued negotiations was the outbreak of the general strike, or rather the mistaken belief of the Government that it had broken out. If that adds to the gravity of the Government's mistake it also adds to the assurance that the general strike never has been and is not now the consequence of an insurmountable difficulty over the economic problem of the mines. We publish to-day for the first time the exact phrasing of the formula submitted by the Government to the T.U.C. for the continuance of the mining negotiations, on the basis of an extended subsidy, the withdrawal of the mining notices and a reduction of wages. Is this formula still open? Evidently not, until the general strike orders are withdrawn. But if in fact the formula represents what both the Government and the T.U.C. are still willing to accept, then the general strike has no meaning; the T.U.C. is fighting because it cannot face the humiliation of surrender, and the Government because it feels that it cannot negotiate or come to terms with an unconstitutional force; but there is no difference between them as to the terms upon which a provisional settlement is possible over the original cause of dispute which lay, of course, solely within the mining industry. That is a situation which ought not to be allowed to continue. The country ought to know definitely what it is that the T.U.C. is fighting for, beyond saving its face, and whether the Government's formula is still open if the general strike orders are withdrawn. Mr. J.H. Thomas has said over and over again that the Government's formula offered a reasonable prospect of peace. If that is the considered view of the T.U.C. then there is not the faintest excuse for the continuance of the general strike for a day longer. Why should not the Government declare that the basis of peace which they offered on Sunday night is still open? And if Mr. Thomas speaks for the T.U.C. what possible reason could that body have for not cancelling the strike notices on the strength of it?

DISTURBANCES.

BUS SET ON FIRE IN STREET.

Yesterday morning a mob of men attacked 'buses near the Elephant and Castle, London, and set fire to one. The volunteer driver and conductor were forced to get off, and were roughly handled in their retreat. The 'bus blazed fiercely. Police galloped to the scene and foot constables and specials soon had the situation in hand. The brigade took a considerable time to quell the flames.

On the Elephant and Castle Corner another bus was waylaid and the driver and conductor had to flee to safety. The 'bus nearly crashed into a public house. In the commotion a van was nearly upset, and it is stated that a motor-cyclist broke his arm. There is a strong force of police at the corner.

Further towards Blackfriars a Ford van was overturned and lay in the line of the traffic for some time.

BUS WRECKED: MAN KILLED.

London Police courts to-day reflected scenes of disturbance

arising out of the strike. A 'bus collided with a motor-cycle and cart, and mounted the pavement at the Elephant and Castle, killing a man.

George Crudington (21), of Southwark, who was alleged to have thrown a half-wooden block at the 'bus, was remanded for a week at the Tower Bridge police court.

'You are entitled to strike if you like, but you must strike peacably,' said the Lambeth Magistrates when fining Albert John Sibley Keys (39), a labourer, of Camberwell, London, for throwing an advertisement board through the window of a tramcart.

For throwing a brick at a tramcar another man got two months' hard labour, and another man 21 days for obstructing a tram driver.

Wm. Nourse, a tram driver, was sentenced to three weeks in the second division for throwing missiles at a tramcar; and for striking a sub-inspector with a bottle, a labourer named Wm. Titchener got six months' hard labour.

The majority of forty-four cases at Lambeth arose out of scenes, in Camberwell and the New Kent-road. Cases at Old Street included assaults on police, stone throwing and preventing the use of a food lorry. The next London court dealt with forty 'strike' cases.

Between 70 and 80 L.G.O.C. 'buses failed to return to the depots by the scheduled time on Wednesday owing to damage received in various parts of London.

MR. SAKLATVALA.
Refuses to be Bound Over

Mr. Saklatvala, the communist M.P. for North Battersea, refused to be bound over for 12 months, when he again appeared to-day at Bowstreet to show cause why he should not find a surety for his good behaviour. The alternative was two months' imprisonment. The proceedings arose out of the May Day speech delivered by Mr. Saklatvala in Hyde Park.

Mr. Saklatvala said that he accepted the fairness and accuracy of the report of his speech, except in regard to punctuation in two places. 'I consider myself,' he said, 'just as unnecessarily called upon to be bound over as our Prime Minister might be. It was never my intention either at this meeting or in any of my propaganda work to incite any sort of disorder or encourage any sort of breach of the peace.'

Sir Chartres Biron, in announcing his decision said: 'I have no doubt whatever in my mind that this is a seditious speech calculated to provoke disorder. In such a critical moment of public affairs, to inflame public opinion by such a delivery is an act of criminal folly. I shall bind you over to keep the peace and to be of good behaviour for twelve months in the sum of £500. I shall require two sureties of £250, or you must go to prison for two months.'

The defendant: 'In my honour and conscience I cannot accept the decision to be bound over.' (A voice in court cried 'Hear, hear!' but there was no further demonstration.)

Sir Charles said that was a special division to which people were committed in default of finding sureties, but he could not take any distinction of the law in this case. There was no demonstration outside the court when the case concluded.

LABOUR STIFFENING.
Mr. Macdonald & Mr. Thomas Rebuked.

(From our Labour Correspondent.)

London, Thursday.

There is a strong feeling on the trade union side that Mr. Macdonald and Mr. J.H. Thomas in their speeches in the House of Commons have gone a little too far in 'grovelling for peace,' as Mr. Thomas puts it.

It is felt that as the Government has stiffened the unions must stiffen too. The General Trades Council, the Labour Party and the Miners' Executive in the two last meetings to-day have indicated plainly to the Parliamentary leaders that they are not expected to be apologetic any longer.

THE WORKERS' OFFICIAL NEWSPAPER.

No. 1 of the 'British Worker,' published by the General Council of the Trade Unions Congress on Wednesday evening, is an eight-page sheet, four narrow columns to a page of approximately 'Daily Herald' size. Prominent on the front page is the following 'message to all workers:'

The General Council of the Trades Union Congress wishes to emphasise the fact that this is an industrial dispute. It expects every member taking part to be exemplary in his conduct, and not to give any opportunity for police interference. The outbreak of any disturbances would be very damaging to the prospects of a successful termination of the dispute. The Council asks pickets especially to avoid obstruction, and to confine themselves strictly to their legitimate duties.

The articles clearly indicate the growing divisions within the ranks of the labour movement. Clearly the TUC were suspicious of the Labour Party's anxiety to maintain its credibility as a 'responsible' force in British politics by quickly ending the strike. The TUC was also, however, under pressure from its rank and file intoxicated by their initial success and wanting to increase the pressure on the Government.

OPINION ABROAD.

(From our own Correspondents.)

GERMANY.

Berlin, Thursday.

Berlin Press publishes utterly confused accounts of the British strike. The conservative papers try to create the impression that the strike has already collapsed. The Communist 'Rote Fahne' writes as though the general strike was absolutely complete, volunteer organisations amounted to nothing and England were almost in a state of civil war. If it were not for 'Vorwaerts', with its remarkably objective enlightening despatches from London and Berlin, the press would leave one almost entirely in the dark about events in England. The German Christian Miners' Union, a relatively Conservative organisation which held aloof until yesterday, came to the same decisions as Socialist unions at Essen yesterday evening so that almost the entire German labour movement has declared itself in favour of every measure possible to help the British strikers.

FRANCE.

Paris, Thursday.

Reasonable opinion in France, irrespective of parties, is becoming restive, petulant at the prospect of the indefinite continuation of the struggle in England, which seems in French eyes a meaningless conflict of prestige that is shaking the whole economic edifice of Europe, and has already sent the Franc toppling down. Of course, besides the Fascists, no one here takes the revolutionary bogey seriously. Political credit remains even firmer than the pound sterling, but the credit of British intelligence has fallen very low.

Mr. Pierre Bertrand, in 'Quotidien' says: 'Neither side wanted this fight in England. Both blundered into it. Let the English people ask themselves whether the whole future of their country is not endangered in this conflict, which no one wanted or willed, but for which the carelessness, indifference and insouciance of all parties is responsible.'

ITALY.

Rome, Thursday.

The strike continues deeply to interest the opinion of the press here. Fascist 'Impero' thinks it is a sure sign of the downfall of the British Empire, which will make room for rising Italian Empire. The Communist 'Unita' stresses the new revolutionary spirit that it sees in the British proletariat. The British middle classes see Moscow's hands in the strike, but the truth is graver, for it is Moscow's spirit now possessing the strikers, hitherto corrupted by the reformism of Macdonald and Thomas. Only the blind fail to receive the rule of English capitalists, whom Trotsky rightly calls civilised vampires, as nearly over. 'Avanti' gravely stresses the vital importance of the outcome of the strike, because the defeat of the English workers means defeat of the whole European proletariat with intensification of the prevailing sad conditions. It does not suggest victory as possible, but praises the strikers for having the courage to lay hands on industry's running sore, namely, the urgent need to re-organise production on broader and humaner bases.

Saturday May 8 1926

THE STRIKE ILLEGAL.
Warning by Sir John Simon.

(From our Political Correspondent.)

London, Friday.

The talk of the House of Commons to-day was an important speech by Sir John Simon, defining the legal and also the Liberal view of the general strike. The speech was made very late at night, too late for most newspapers or newspaper substitutes, although its principal point was reported in the 'Manchester Guardian' this morning.

Sir John Simon said that this general strike was not a strike at all. It was really very different. A strike, properly understood, was perfectly lawful. It was an essential part of the rights of the British wage-earner that he should have the right to strike, which ought never to be taken away from him. Those who really appreciated the character of British institutions would never wish to take it away from him.

The decision of the trade union representatives to call out everybody, regardless of the contracts which these workmen have made, was not a lawful act at all. Every workman bound by contract to give notice before he left work who, in view of the decision either of his own freewill or because he felt compelled, had left work by leaving his employment without proper notice, had broken the law just as the coalowners would have done if they had broken the wages agreement without notice. It would be lamentable if the working-classes of this country did not understand that they were taking part in an utterly illegal proceeding.

Every railwayman, for example, was himself personally liable to be sued in the County Court for damages. Every trade union leader who had advised and permitted that course of action was liable in damages to the uttermost farthing of his personal possessions. Sir John Simon then referred to the fear of men called out on strike that if they refused they would forfeit the benefits to which they were entitled from their trade union in its capacity of a friendly society. 'Any rule,' he said, 'laying down that a trade unionist forfeits his benefits if he does not obey the order of his executive means and only means that he may so forfeit those benefits if the order is lawful.'

Sir John deliberately declared the legal position to be that a man could not be deprived of his benefits for refusing an order to commit an unlawful act. This, he said, could not be too widely known. Sir John described the proclamation of a general strike as a tragic blunder which deprived the miners of proper sympathy and put in jeopardy the rights of organised labour. The day would come when this strike was ended – could be ended – when an irritated, resentful suffering nation would be asked to make an immense revision and reduction of the rights of organised labour, and the people who were responsible were the very people whose duty it was at all costs to have told the working classes that a general strike was a very different thing from an ordinary strike.

Sir John Simon added that when that reaction came he would support the legitimate rights of trade unionists.

This speech was particularly significant coming from a respected barrister and former Home Secretary. Simon's ruling that the strike was illegal intensified the belief within the TUC that a solution must be sought and gave further urgency to the contacts with Sir Herbert Samuel (see 'Chronology of Main Events').

HOUSE OF COMMONS.

The House yesterday spent two hours in peaceful discussion of a number of small bills, but afterwards on the formal motion for the adjournment of the House there were one or two displays of angry feeling. The strike has spread to the staff of the House. The Speaker said he regretted that the men engaged on the principal services of the House had been withdrawn, but he would not allow it to be disabled from proceeding with its work. If it became necessary he would conduct the business of the House without any printing and without any electric light.

Considerable resentment was aroused among Labour members by a request by Sir Gerald Strickland that special effort should be made to print a speech delivered in the House late on Thursday evening by Sir J. Simon dealing, it is understood, with certain legal aspects of the general strike. Cries of protest were raised on the government benches as Mr. Lansbury launched out into the charge against the Prime Minister and his Cabinet colleagues of breaking-off peace negotiations on a mere subterfuge. To shouts of 'nonsense' Mr. Lansbury exclaimed 'I appeal to Hansard. The Prime Minister himself said he broke off negotiations because half-a-dozen men refused to print that miserable rag the "Daily Mail." '

STRIKE ITEMS.

John Harrison (26) of Brentford, was sent to prison for a month yesterday for throwing a pair of pliers through a window of a tramcar which was being used for instructing volunteers at Twickenham.

Facilities for the distribution of food supplies were withdrawn from Messrs. J. Lyons and Co. Ltd. on Thursday night by the Workers' Union. A large percentage of the transport and distributing staff at Cadby Hall withdrew. The following notice was posted up yesterday by the management – 'Staff not reporting for their duties before 12 noon Saturday, May 8th, will have their jobs filled.'

Twenty-five thousand volunteers were enrolled in London and the Home Counties on Thursday, making a total of seventy-five thousand.

Men at the Durham electricity power station have come out, but the work is being carried on by volunteers.

The Government points out that circulation of alarmist rumours such as savings banks ceasing payment and mutiny, is a criminal offence.

Isobel Brown, married, a certificated teacher, whose last permanent address was Moscow, was committed for three months at Pontefract yesterday for sedition. It was alleged that she addressed a crowd at Castleford appealing to the Forces not to act against the workers.

NO SYMPATHETIC STRIKE ON THE CONTINENT.

Paris 'Journal' states that in well-informed labour quarters it is affirmed that neither the French, Belgian nor German miners appear ready to declare a general strike in order to support the particular claims of the British miners. The most that can be expected is that the Continental miners may agree to a 24 hours protest strike on condition that they receive financial assistance.

STONING AND LOOTING IN GLASGOW.

POLICE CHARGES.

(From our Special Correspondents.)

Glasgow, Friday.

Eighty-nine men appeared at the Eastern Police Court to-day, charged with riotous conduct and breaches of the peace. Most were arrested in the early hours of the morning during encounters with the police in the East End of the city, where the lawless spirit developed strongly after dark on Thursday. After the tramcars ceased running the rumour spread that student volunteers were lodged at the tram depot ready to take the cars out in the morning. A mob of men marched on the depot with the object of evicting the students. There was a great deal of stone throwing, and the police made several charges, using their truncheons freely and making a number of arrests.

While the disturbance was in progress hooligans broke a number of shop windows and looted the goods. A small public house was broken into and liquor stolen. In one of the rushes a youth of twenty was pushed through a shop window and was cut so severely about the body that he had to be taken to hospital.

About one o'clock this afternoon a mob of men went to the Students' Union and invited the students out to fight. The police dispersed the mob by truncheon charges. Rioters boarded a tram which had arrived at the University terminus and removed the control lever. A student driver, who tried to resist the men, was struck on the face with the lever and partially stunned.

There are 190 cars running to-day, about fifty more than yesterday. The Corporation motor-buses are reappearing in the streets. In some districts they are stoned as they pass, and there have been one or two instances of injury to passengers, happily of a minor character only.

Cardiff, Friday.

Full Corporation 'bus service now working in Cardiff and many electric trams. Apart from railway transport traffic situation almost normal. Railway situation improving. Throughout South Wales a surprising orderliness is maintained. There have been small disturbances here and there, 'buses and trams having proved provocative things. Cardiff strikers have tried to stop them, always unsuccessfully and to-day the men became so menacing and assembled in such numbers that police cleared streets with truncheons. All things considered, however, situation extraordinarily placid.

POLICE CHARGE AT HULL.

Owing to the hostile attitude of strikers towards volunteers recruiting at the City Hall, Hull, the police made a truncheon charge yesterday afternoon. Seven people were injured and one or two innocent people hurt. Mounted police endeavoured to disperse a crowd of 3,000 in the City Square, and eventually a truncheon charge was made and the Square cleared. One or two arrests were made.

EDINBURGH RIOTERS SENT TO PRISON.

About 20 men and three women were dealt with by the Sheriff, yesterday, at Edinburgh, on charges arising out of Thursday's rioting. One man was sent to prison for 40 days, a number received 30 days, and the remainder were fined from one to three pounds.

The Chief Constable of Birmingham says gangs of men have forcibly held up 'buses and charabancs. Engines have been interfered with, and tyres punctured. Some drivers have been threatened.

POWER STATION WORKERS.

The Home Office yesterday evening announced:—

'The situation remains unchanged and the country is quiet generally. In London concerted action by strikers to prevent the transport of food by road continues but the situation is being dealt with. In the provinces attempts are also being made to cut off the supply of electricity for essential services by calling out men from power stations. Strikers are, however, being replaced successfully.'

When Wrexham miners commenced picking coal from the pit banks yesterday with the intention of selling it, railwaymen threatened to return to the railways, and the miners desisted.

THE ARMED FORCES.

GOVERNMENT ANNOUNCEMENT TO ALL RANKS.

The following announcement is made by His Majesty's Government:

'All ranks – the armed forces of the Crown – are hereby notified that any action they may find it necessary to take in an

73

honest endeavour to aid the civil power will receive both now and afterwards the full support of H.M. Government.'

OMINOUS GOVERNMENT ANNOUNCEMENT.

The 'Official Communique' in to-day's 'British Gazette' is headed 'Organised attempt to starve the nation.'

The communique contains the following:—

The situation is becoming more intense, and the climax is not yet reached. Orders have been sent by the leaders of the railway and transport trade unions to do their utmost to paralyse and break down the supply of food and the necessaries of life.

Intimidation, both by disorderly crowds and pickets has occurred in many places and may soon occur in many more. H.M. Government have directed all authorities to repress and overcome these criminal obstructions. The recruitment of special constables in all parts of the country is being vigorously and rapidly pressed forward.

It is proposed to raise the numbers of special constables in London as quickly as possible to 50,000. Other important measures to increase the forces at the disposal of the Government, and to enable widespread protection to be afforded are also being taken.

An organised attempt is being made to starve the people, and to wreck the State.

STRINGENT ORDERS FROM T.U.C.

(From our Labour Correspondent.)

London, Friday.

To-night's Government communication denounces the trade union's attempt 'to paralyse and break down the supply of food and necessaries of life.' The National Union of Railwaymen has now ordered that its members 'must handle no traffic of any kind, foodstuffs or otherwise,' and the transport committee of the General Council has ordered its local committees to review all permits which have been issued. This is done, it is said, because of the Government's refusal, because of the 'gross abuse of permits which have been issued by committees,' and because of 'the attitude adopted by certain police authorities in declaring that the permits already issued are illegal.'

Similar conflict is arising on the electricity supply. Local strike organisations are 'authorised to meet employers' and offer to supply light and power for house, street and shop lighting, social services, power for food, bakeries, laundries and domestic

74

purposes. Power for industrial purposes is barred. Some authorities are said to have accepted the offer – probably the London Labour Authorities. In most the distinction cannot be maintained.

INTERFERENCE WITH TRANSPORT.

BEGINNING OF VIOLENCE.

(From our Political Correspondent.)

London, Friday.

It is inferred from reports received by the Government from all over the country that in the last day or two the tactics of the strikers have changed towards volunteer transport and that they are now entering upon a definite policy of hampering the transport of food and other supplies by more or less violent obstruction. It is believed that the T.U.C. has ceased to issue the permits of which some traders availed themselves, and that existing permits have been cancelled. The Government claims to be prepared for a possible stoppage of gas and electricity works, though it is not pretended that there would not be some interruption of supply.

To protect people who use the emergency road services, the authorities are putting more and more constables and special constables on that duty.

THE GENERAL STRIKE NOTICES.

Reply of T.U.C. to the Premier.

The reply of the General Council of the T.U.C. to the Prime Minister's statement as to the possible terms includes the following, as it appears in 'The British Worker': 'At this stage, with no knowledge of the subsequent line of policy that the Government intend to pursue, the General Council cannot comply with Prime Minister's request for an unconditional withdrawal of the notices for the general strike. The General Council, while ready at any moment to resume negotiations for an honourable settlement, gives an unqualified "no" to the Premier's request for an unconditional withdrawal of the strike notices. The Government was responsible for breaking off the negotiations, and any further discussions can only be undertaken in a free and unfettered atmosphere.'

Dealing with the charges of interfering with motor 'buses in Hammersmith Broadway, the West London magistrate said such an offence could now be dealt with under the Emergency Powers

Act by a sentence of three months' imprisonment. 'Women will be treated the same as men,' he added. 'They often inflame men's passions.'

NO NEGOTIATIONS.

(From our Labour Correspondent.)

London, Friday.

The General Council of the T.U.C. denies all reports of negotiations. 'No official or unofficial overtures have been made to the Government by any individual or group of individuals, either with or without the sanction of the General Council,' which has had 'no direct or indirect conversation with the Government since last Monday. The Council is ready at any moment to enter into preliminary discussions regarding the withdrawal of the lock-out notices, and to ending of the general stoppage and the resumption of negotiation for an honourable settlement of the mining dispute. These preliminary discussions must be free from any condition.'

Crowd about 4,000 prevented closing of level-crossing gates at Middlesbrough station. On arrival of police crowd rushed gates and two police officers were stoned. Lorries chained to lines, and naval ratings from gunboat called out. Another demonstration outside police station. 'Bus attacked and windows smashed. 'Bus service discontinued. – At Newark train held up at level-crossing by strikers, who were dispersed by police.

The L.M.S. Railway state practically whole of station staffs have returned to duty at Goostrey, Chelford, Alderley Edge, Handforth and Cheadle Hulme.

Captain Amundsen's airship, the Norge, arrived at King's Bay, Spitzbergen yesterday.

'Bus services were maintained between Clitheroe, Blackburn and Accrington until Thursday night, when, owing to the increasing hostility displayed by the strikers, the 'buses were withdrawn.

Sheffield is threatened with a beer famine, the carters having been called out.

WILL THE KING INTERVENE?

(From our London Correspondent.)

London, Friday.

In the continued rain, the hardships and discomforts of the strike were brought home to Londoners, most of whom cannot use the tube services and electric train services now running and having little chance of a ride on the overcrowded 'buses. City workers living seven or eight miles from their business and having to walk are showing the strain. Still apart from the decreased traffic, the city looks much as usual, except for the anxious crowds around the news bulletins as they are put up. 'Are they in touch?' is the common question, but neither the T.U.C. nor the Government have given any sign.

One rumour, much in the London spirit, that has got about, is that the King is going to ask both sides to tea at the Palace. It is said that the bishops of Winchester and of Southwark have approached the King with the proposal, the plan being that as neither side can ask to meet the other at this juncture without it being thought a sign of weakness, the King is the only one who could bring them together without prejudice to either side.

A conciliation tea party at Buckingham Palace to end a national strike would indeed make history. Foreign observers are amazed by the general peacefulness, apart from the few tram and 'bus incidents in the outer quarters. Men are disputing together at street corners, and in taverns, without fisticuffs, and the casualty list is still under a hundred, with no fatalities so far as is known and no use of firearms.

The two main incidents to-day are the strike payments by the unions – some of whom are said to be finding difficulty in the immediate realisation of their funds as is natural with any big stock selling at this time. The other is that many industrial firms yesterday and to-day have had to give notice to their workers, as their goods and raw materials are stopped by the transport strike, and they cannot carry on. The consequences at the end of next week, when factories shut down and the strikers are feeling the heavier pinch of households on strike pay, will mean that the iron phase of the strike has come.

Already the restaurant and dancing life of West London has almost stopped, for people hurry home at night, and there are no taxi-cabs.

Monday May 10 1926

Leader **TOWARDS PEACE.**

It is just a week since Civil War was declared in this country. It is not a war of arms; it is not yet even a war of tempers; it is a trial of strength. The struggle is unequal because the resources of the State are greater than those of any section of its citizens and because also the engines used against the State are all boomerangs; not one can be launched without recoiling with deadly effect on the engineers. They are broadly speaking unemployment and starvation. Who suffers from unemployment and starvation?

We are all asking ourselves how did it, how could it begin; how soon, by what means can it be ended? Some people say: 'No; we are in for a fight; fight it out; everything else will keep.' That way lies madness. Of course we must fight it out. For the State to submit to any power other than its own would be suicide. But not to admit error and to repair it, if error there be, and not to seek peace all the time would be no less a failure in courage and in duty. To begin with let us confess right out what Mr. Baldwin has in so many words admitted himself that the breakdown took place on a simple and patent misunderstanding. He and his Cabinet thought the General Strike had begun; it had not begun. Some wholly unauthorised people had committed an act of violence in a single newspaper office. They were instantly repudiated. To break off negotiations which had actually almost succeeded was an act of ignorance and panic. As such it ought to be confessed and it ought to be repaired.

How can it be repaired? Such things unhappily are vastly easier to do than to undo. Nevertheless the task must be attempted and the effort must never for a moment be relaxed. Duty demands it, self-respect demands it, the vital interests of the State and above all of the poorest of the citizens demand it. The primary difficulty is that the strike is now in force. It must be ended, we are told, before negotiations can begin. Taken literally that would mean what is called a fight to a finish; in this case a trial of endurance lasting certainly for weeks, possibly for months, with damage material, moral and political, unimaginable and running far into the future, perhaps changing the whole hearty and healthy relations of classes in this country and making Moscow class war for the first time possible. It must not be.

There are possibilities, we cannot pretend to exhaust them. It is the business of the strongest, the wisest and the sanest heads and of all men of goodwill to consider and to help. Why not begin where negotiation ended? If we cannot negotiate formally why not informally? If there is no longer, as would seem to be the case, any difference of substance between the parties why not make that clear, as it would have been made clear on the fatal Sunday night had not the wretched irrelevance of the 'Daily Mail' incident intervened? Or, if that be refused, why should not the King take a hand and call the parties – all of them – together? He could do no greater service to the people of his Kingdom.

There are various means of approach; any, or all, should be attempted. The one foolish and fatal thing is to let the forces which have been let loose go forward unchecked and undirected to their own destructive end.

A TIME TABLE.

We publish to-day an exact time-table of the events which ended in the breakdown of the negotiations on Sunday last week. It confirms in detail the accounts which have already appeared and it is not likely that history will have much more to add. All the chief actors in the drama substantially agree in their stories. Everyone can now form his own judgment on the vital questions at issue – whether the government were right to break off negotiations at that particular moment, whether the incident at the 'Daily Mail' offices was an adequate occasion for breaking them off, whether the negotiations, if pursued, would be likely to have resulted in agreement and whether the stage which was then reached is the most promising basis for resumed negotiations, when these again become possible.

TIME-TABLE OF BREAKDOWN.

(From our Political Correspondent.)

There has been so much confusion about exact sequence of events that ended in the breakdown on Sunday night that it may be useful to state the time-table of the critical hours.

The three Cabinet Ministers met the three T.U.C. negotiators at number 10 Downing Street at 9-10 p.m. They sat until 10-55. The Ministers then went to confer with full cabinet who were waiting next door, and T.U.C. representatives went to consult their colleagues, who were at the Treasury. The miners had not then arrived. T.U.C. representatives did not see miners until 12 or later. Meanwhile action of N.S.O.P.A. in suppressing 'Daily Mail' had come to knowledge of Cabinet. Cabinet broke up about 12-30, and about 12-45 Premier gave the letter breaking off negotiations to Thomas. It was not till 1-30 that Thomas sought Premier again, presumably to convey T.U.C.'s repudiation of action taken against 'Daily Mail.' It was then that Thomas found everyone gone and everything in darkness. It is stated that what happened was that Thomas found a messenger, who said the Premier had gone to bed. Thomas pressed no further. It was true that Premier had gone to bed, but his four Private Secretaries were still waiting in No. 10. Thomas did not know this, and did not ask to see the Secretaries, nor press to have any message conveyed to Premier.

STRIKE ITEMS.

Gang set fire to motor-bus at Newington. Police have raided office at Shipley (West Riding) where seditious literature was being produced. Bradford textile mills are working. Hereford gasworkers, who threatened to strike have withdrawn threat and are working satisfactorily. Three Cambridge students at Poole with 25-ton cutter offer to carry anybody or anything within their capacity across the Channel.

Canister of explosive detonated by train in Durham county. Crowd attempted to rush police station at Preston to rescue man charged with throwing. Six arrests in truncheon charge. Hull trams and 'buses reappearing yesterday with wire-netting to protect windows. Men from Bangor brought to help on railway at Holyhead attacked.

Expected that volunteers will be able to work ships in Manchester Ship Canal; arrangements being made to accommodate 2,000 men at docks on board ships.

Deptford 'bus driver returning from picket duty found cottage on fire; injured in rescue attempt, and wife and two little children burned to death.

At Liverpool docks 5,300 men engaged unloading 25 steamers. London picket sent to gaol for attempting to hold up food lorries and assaulting police.

Victoria Park (N.E. London) turned into military camp; Regent's Park, as well as Hyde Park, now closed and used for public purposes.

A brick wall was pulled down for ammunition to storm food lorry in Wandsworth, and garden railings torn up in attempt to stop Camberwell tram. Bradford strikers, who refuse information to regular press, publishing own bulletin. In football match at Plymouth, strikers beat police team 2–1. Seventy-five London Underground stations open on Saturday with regular service. Man sentenced North London for saying 'Welsh Guards refused to act,' and '17,000 of Army on strike.' Porter at Marylebone sent to prison for stoning 'bus. Five cases incendiarism in London affecting one bus, three lorries, and one car.

Civil Commissioner report Manchester and Liverpool each about 10,000 volunteers. Bootle and Birkenhead millers disregarding threats to bring out men handling flour. Pickets causing difficulty at Preston, but traders' requirements generally met. Large supplies petrol moved from Hull to Leeds and Newcastle. All reports show coal-fields particularly quiet and miners' conduct exemplary.

As a train for London was passing underneath a bridge near Crewe on Saturday, shots were fired at the driver and fireman. Nobody was struck.

FIGHTING THE MOB IN GLASGOW.

POLICEMAN INJURED.

(From our Special Correspondent.)

Glasgow, Sunday.

Nearly 230 people arrested in Glasgow for riotous conduct since early Friday morning. One batch of 80 were concerned in attack on Tramway depot. This attack was renewed early on Saturday, when about 60 men were taken into custody after baton charges by the police. It is thought this rioting was not caused by strikers but by hooligans.

It began in every case with the looting of shops, boot shops being specially singled out. When police drew baton and charged, they were met with showers of stones, and very vigorous measures were needed.

Three constables were injured so severely that they had to be removed to the infirmary. One of them was violently kicked, and his condition is serious.

THE TRAGIC SIDE.

Cardiff, Sunday.

Praise due to conduct of strikers and police. Only occasional 'bubblings over.' Tram and train services improving daily. Many unemployed finding work at last, particularly on trams, with guarantee of permanent employment. Pitiful to talk with strikers seeing jobs vanishing and yet maintaining half-doubtful loyalty to T.U.C. leaders. Here and there few stealing back to work, and hundreds confess had no idea T.U.C. could thus dispose their fates. All Typographical Association men have returned to 'South Wales News.'

TRAIN STONED: PASSENGERS INJURED.

Further railway outrage near Newcastle on Saturday night, when Morpeth–Newcastle train stoned, several passengers being cut by glass. Signal box set on fire.

Crowd from Gateshead joined Newcastle rowdies in attack on police on Saturday night. Some policemen slightly hurt, but truncheon charge secured control.

SOLDIERS WITH FIXED BAYONETS.

The police had to make truncheon charges in King Edward Street, Hull, on Saturday afternoon owing to stoning of tramcars.

One policeman was injured. Tram and 'bus services continue with volunteer drivers.

At midnight on Saturday, shops were looted in localities from which the police had been drawn. Soldiers with fixed bayonets relieved the police in one district, and a motor fire engine was sent to disperse crowds who were looting elsewhere.

First truncheon charge in Newcastle on Saturday night, after police inspector had been knocked down in crowd and specials on point duty had been chased.

STREET CONFLICTS AT MIDDLESBROUGH.

There were further disturbances late on Saturday night and early yesterday morning at Middlesbrough. Gangs of young hooligans broke loose and smashed windows of shops in several streets. In Newport-road the police, threatened by a hostile mob, made several truncheon charges. These were watched by the Mayor. A woman was pushed through a plate-glass window and injured. In another place in the town a police constable was rendered unconscious. Order was not restored until 2 a.m. yesterday. In all places of worship yesterday morning an appeal was read from the Mayor requesting all persons to be in their homes by dark to assist authorities.

ARMOURED CARS OUT.
Strong Military Escort for Flour.

Two battalions of Guards, a detachment of Cavalry, mounted policemen and armoured cars and a great crowd of volunteers took part in convoying over one hundred lorry loads of flour from Victoria Docks, London, on Saturday. Although it passed through Canning Town, and some of the most disaffected quarters of the East End, the convoy completed its journey without incident.

On Friday two battalions of guards took possession of the docks. Five hundred volunteers were taken to Westminster Pier, and towed in lighters to Victoria Docks.

On Saturday morning over one hundred lorries borrowed from the abundant supply at Hyde Park, and each guarded by two armed soldiers, were driven to the docks. Each lorry was heavily loaded.

The escort on the return journey to Hyde Park was headed by a detachment of mounted police. Then came three armoured cars, while a single car drove between each section of lorries. Four armed soldiers sat on each load of flour sacks, and a squadron of cavalry brought up the rear. The convoy stretched for over two miles, and provided a spectacle that was greeted by large crowds with almost as much enthusiasm as a Lord Mayor's procession. There was no attempt at interference.

Yesterday a second convoy of 150 lorries left the docks under similar escort and took supplies of flour to Hyde Park.

THE GOVERNMENT DISPLAY OF FORCE.

(From our Political Correspondent.)

London, Sunday.

Government intended big convoys of lorries from the docks to Hyde Park as demonstration. Government intend from now on to keep docks open. It is their view that it is policy of strikers to obstruct distribution of goods, including foodstuffs, by intimidation and even violence. Even production of food has been attacked in some cases, as in Liverpool, where flour mill workers have been called out, and in London where attempts have been made to prevent mills from delivering flour to bakers. It is admitted, however, that actual amount of intimidation seems to have been very slight.

There has been no move towards negotiations over week-end. Government has had no indication that unions are prepared to approach them on terms they have laid down; that is, unreserved withdrawal of general strike notices. There can be no question of withdrawal of notices as part of a bargain.

NEW POLICE FORCE FOR LONDON.

It was yesterday officially announced that in addition to the 25,000 men in the Metropolitan Special Constabulary Reserve and the Metropolitan Emergency Constabulary, it has been decided, 'owing to the tactics employed by ill-disposed persons who are taking advantage of the present crisis' to set up a new body, the Civil Constabulary Reserve, to be paid as a whole-time force. Members will wear arm-bands, and steel helmets, and will carry truncheons. Recruits are sought from officers and other ranks of Territorial Army and of the Officers' Training Corps, and ex-military men who can be vouched for at Territorial Association Headquarters, age limit 50. Pay (daily): commander 10/-, inspector 7/6, sergeant 6/-, constable 5/-; -5/- weekly clothing allowance: army rations. Members of Territorial units joining together will serve together in units under their own officers.

MANCHESTER.

Lord Mayor announced yesterday that food supplies are satisfactorily maintained. Man arrested for alleged attempt to interfere with lorry-load of flour from Sutcliffe's mill, Hulme, – this the only incident of kind reported. Several hundred strikers marched to Platt Fields yesterday, where large audiences were addressed by local Labour leaders, including Mr. R.J. Davies, M.P. Additional trains ran from Manchester on Saturday on L.M.S. to Carlisle, Chester, Crewe, London, and Leeds. L.N.E.R. promise goods train to-day from London-road station to London at 9-30. L.M.S. trains to London will leave to-day, 7-15 a.m., 8-0 a.m., 10-30 a.m. and 12-50 p.m. The 8-0 a.m. train will give connections for Holyhead. According to Civil Commissioner's report destroyer sent to port. Two steamers unable to unload.

A WAGE GUARANTEE.

Lewis's Ltd., in reply to allegation that strike is a defence against lowering standard of living, announce to their staff that they will not reduce present basic rate of wages for at least three years. This guarantee will also apply to workmen employed on the new buildings, and to employees in Lewis's clothing and boot factories and their associated companies.

Nord & Pas de Calais (France) mining companies granted 10 per cent wages increase, and 15 per cent addition to bonus given to meet increased cost of living.

LONDON CONCILIATION PRESS SILENCED.

(From our London Correspondent.)

London, Sunday.

Many shops and offices closed on Saturday. Central London two-thirds empty. Some independent 'buses had windows boarded up and wire netting in front of drivers. Two shops near the docks were raided because of profiteering in condensed milk. One evening paper had large force of pretty girls selling their sheet all over West End.

Among journals that have come out in printed form this weekend are 'The New Statesman' and 'The Architect.' No Liberal newspapers are appearing in London, so printers' strike has silenced side of press here favourable to conciliation, while nearly all Conservative press is appearing.

GOVERNMENT REVIEW OF SITUATION.

Government spokesman in review of situation yesterday said no material change. Railway transport and other services working smoothly in main; local instances of intimidation and interference with transport. Official assurance given that news not being held back and that, in event of any serious happening, public will be informed fully and at once. Reserve is maintained, however, on location of foodstocks, petrol and other necessaries.

Practically all factories in Walthamstow area idle through cutting off of electric power. Union men at Islington Borough electric power station, having ceased work without notice, dismissed and replaced by volunteers. Three big electric power stations at Newcastle are maintained by volunteers, and South Shields Corporation is maintaining supplies to all consumers. In South Midlands Division some shortage of supplies, particularly groceries. In South Wales Labour has set up councils of action in several areas.

WORKERS PROTECTED.
Premier's New Assurance.

The following notice is printed in yesterday's 'Official Gazette,' and has been circulated by broadcast and placard:–

Additional Guarantees: Every man who does his duty by the country and remains at work or returns to work during the present crisis will be protected by the State from loss of trade union benefits, superannuation allowances or pensions. H.M. Government will take whatever steps are necessary in Parliament or otherwise for this purpose. – Stanley Baldwin.

Only five men responded to a strike call on Saturday night among 'bus employees at Altrincham, the remaining 660 refusing to come out. All employees of Plymouth daily paper are back.

RETURNS TO WORK.

At Chelford five signalmen and two gangs of platelayers are back; also one signalman at Alderley Edge, and another at Handforth. Among others back are Cambridge printers and bookbinders; tramwaymen at Portsmouth; Messrs. J. Lyon's workmen; Yarmouth electricity workers; Southampton, Cardiff and Lowestoft tramway workers.

The L.M.S.R. announce station-masters, controllers, clerks, inspectors and signalmen returning to work. Over 44,000 originally remained loyal. On L.N.E.R. 550 signalmen returned. Total men on duty on Southern Railway now 12,014. Strikers back at Sowerby Bridge and Elland. Seventy-five London Underground stations now able to run regular service. All Typographical Association men at 'South Wales Daily News,' Cardiff, returned.

SEAMEN'S LEADER AND T.U.C.

In message to masters, all ships in British merchant service, Mr. Havelock Wilson (President of the Seamen's Union) says: 'Please read to your crew: unauthorised persons calling seamen out; they say on instructions from T.U.C. They have no authority. Council of your union only body who has power to do so, and then only after members balloted. Hope to have ballot completed Thursday or Friday next. If in favour of strike it is my duty to inform you that courts of law will declare no strike money can be paid from union funds for sympathetic strikers.'

LABOUR PEACE TERMS.
Cancel Lock-out as Well as Strike Order.

(From our Labour Correspondent.)

London, Sunday.

Trade unions put much hope in line of conciliation opened up by message of Archbishop of Canterbury and other leaders of churches suggesting a return to position of Friday week before general strike was declared.

Commenting on Mr. Baldwin's speech last night, Council notes his reference to round-table conference if general strike order is withdrawn. 'We do not find anything in the speech about a condition that the mineowners should withdraw their lockout notices. If, as Premier says, the door is not closed it is for Government to make it clear that lockout notices should be withdrawn as well as general strike order. Negotiations could then take place where they were left last Friday week.'

General Council, in reply to Sir John Simon, does not comment on the legal aspects of his speech, but reiterates that 'in exercising their legal and well-established right of withholding their labour' the unions are doing it only to protect miners against a degradation of their standard of life. The fact that contracts may in some cases have been broken cannot, with any show of reason make the strike other than purely industrial.'

General Council, it says, 'in its anxiety to convince the public that it is not pursuing anything in the nature of a revolutionary struggle' is refusing offers of money from abroad. The All Russian

Central Council of Trade Unions has sent a cheque for some thousands (though not for the £238,000 which the Paris messages report.) This has been returned.

THE LAW AND THE STRIKE.

It may be doubted whether the full importance of the statement of law authoritatively made by Sir John Simon in the House on Thursday is even yet fully appreciated. It amounts to this. The lightning strike being itself illegal, no instructions given by the trade unions to enforce it will hold good in law. No member of a trade union disregarding them therefore and continuing to remain at work can be deprived in consequence of any of his union benefits. He is exactly as free as if no instructions had been given him. Trade unionists may, or may not, desire to act on this liberty, but, having been called out without being consulted, it may naturally and properly influence their decision.

MR. THOMAS ON HIS POSITION.
Against Principle of General Strike.

Speaking at Hammersmith yesterday, Mr. J.H. Thomas, M.P., said that, whatever the end, so far as the nation was concerned it must be worse after the strike than before it. 'I have never disguised, and I do not disguise to-day, that I have never been in favour of the principle of a general strike.' No one would disagree, however, that fundamental principle of trade unionism was not only the right to organise to protect economic interests, but an essential part of the legal right was collective bargaining. Workers had no rights to say to the employer 'You must negotiate under threat of a strike.' But it was equally right that workers should not be asked to carry on negotiations under the threat of lock-out. When T.U.C. first met Government they urged them to force coalowners to withdraw their notices. For a fortnight they pleaded upon that issue, but failed. In spite of all that has been said and all that will be said I repeat that it is the duty of both sides to keep the door open. All attempts to raise the constitutional issue are dangerous. Whatever the result it will not be made by us a challenge to the constitution. Even if they won every point in the miners' position and beat the Government on that question, there was not a member of the General Council who would dare to say their object was to supersede constitutional Government. 'The task is a difficult one: responsibility is indeed a heavy one. But there will be a graver responsibility on whichever side fails to recognise the moment when an honourable settlement can be arrived at. The moment must be accepted, and everyone must work to that end.'

THE PRIMATE.

Archbishop of Canterbury, in sermon broadcast last night, denied Churches were helpless or apathetic. Referred to Church Leaders' Concordat proposal issued by himself on Friday and reaffirmed belief that first step towards resumption of negotiations must be on these lines. Duty of Christians having elected leaders and given them power, to be firmly and even sternly loyal to them and law and order.

The basis of concordat suggested by Primate was as follows:—

Return to *status quo* of Friday last, the proposal involving simultaneously: (1) T.U.C. cancellation of strike; (2) renewal of government offer of assistance to mines for short period; (3) mineowners' withdrawal of new wages scale recently issued.

SPORT.

CRICKET: Australia 301 (6) v. Surrey; Lancs. 145 (Hallows 50), Gloucester 79 (1); Yorks. 170, Derby 76 (2); Essex 246 (Russell 122 n.o.), Middlesex 5 (0); Worcester 223, Somerset 14 (2); Warwick 266 (Parsons 171), Hants 16 (2); Notts. 232 (G. Gunn 114), Sussex 62 (4); Leicester 195, Glamorgan 37 (1).

FOOTBALL – Manchester, Cup (final): Manchester U. 2, Manchester City 0.

NORTHERN UNION (League championship): Wigan 22 pts. Warrington 10.

LAWN TENNIS: Turnbull and Wheatley won Davis Cup singles against Poland at Harrogate.

Tuesday May 11 1926

HOW THE WORLD SEES US.
The Few Casualties.

(From our London Editor.)

Fleet Street, Monday.

To see strike in perspective, one must talk to Foreign and Dominion correspondents in London. American correspondents alone are sending about 40,000 words a night, and long cables are going to Canada and Australia. What impresses them most is that number of casualties at Joan of Arc celebration riots in Paris on Sunday were greater than casualties in National Strike in

England. Another point is that after the war, with Englishmen for first time generally used to firearms and warfare, it was feared that industrial troubles would assume vast increase of violence. Present troubles up to now have been unprecedented in temper shown by the strikers. Unselfish motives, who brought out vast majority of strikers to suffer hardship and to risk their livelihoods, have also much impressed itself on these observers.

NEW INDEPENDENT NEWSPAPER IN LONDON.

(From our London Correspondent.)

London, Monday.

Whatever idea of calling out printers, result is more and more clear. 'The British Worker' is now reduced to very small double sheet. London Liberal papers have been completely stopped, while Government official paper and London papers that support Government are all appearing in one form or another. Liberal opinion alone that would make for conciliation and criticism has been silenced in London.

Attempts are at last being made to place London Liberal press on level of other papers. One of the London dailies is expected to appear to-morrow, and another is contemplating resuscitation, and there is also likelihood of Liberal newcomer. Besides this, a non-party paper produced to provide the platform for conciliation, which is not elsewhere adequately supplied in London, will appear to-morrow, entitled: 'The British Independent'. It is staffed by Oxford undergraduates, and should be a powerful mediator in the struggle for peace.

NEWSPAPERS PUBLISHED.

Leeds newspapers appear as usual, 'Yorkshire Post' office producing over 700,000 and serving from Carlisle to Manchester and North East coast. Emergency editions published yesterday by 'Times,' 'Daily Telegraph,' 'Daily Express,' 'Daily Mirror,' 'Daily Mail,' 'Daily Graphic,' 'London Evening News,' 'Manchester Evening News.'

'Gloucester Citizen,' 'Hereford Times' (publishing daily), 'Accrington Observer' (8 pages), 'South Wales Argus,' 'Northern Echo,' 'Sunday Mercury,' 'Birmingham Gazette,' 'Independent' and the 'Evening Mail' (Sheffield), 'Nottingham Evening News,' journals at Swindon, Norwich, Lincoln, Lancaster and Durham. Owing to applications of staff to return, 'Daily Express' contemplates reissue in its normal form.

RETURNS TO WORK.
Birmingham Services Improving.

Appears worst of transport hold-up at Birmingham now over. Two tram routes reopened to-day with returned men; remainder given till Wednesday to return. More trains and 'buses. Industry, though handicapped by no means paralysed. Gas and electricity supplies normal; plenty of volunteers if needed. City remarkably quiet. Labour councillor remanded yesterday in connection with speech alleged likely to cause disaffection.

Railway goods clerks and shipyard workers returned at Workington. Trains as usual at Leeds, Dewsbury, Edinburgh. More at Huddersfield, Glasgow, Birmingham, and Liverpool. L.N.E.R. reports 616 signal boxes open; 28,000 men on duty includes 603 strikers. Hull fish workers refuse to strike; all ships unloaded.

Fifth of railway staffs at work.

Printers at Bristol, Hinckley, Galashiels, Maidstone and Middleton (where papers will publish as usual). Binders at Whitehaven, Carlisle and Norwich, Dundee and Bath tramwaymen.

Staffs of 'Thanet Advertiser,' 'Stroud Journal,' 'Gloucester Citizen,' half T.A. members on 'Accrington Observer,' 'Weston-Super-Mare Mercury,' 'South Wales Argus,' are back. Many 'Daily Express' men applied for re-instatement.

Bury Tramway Employees requested by committee to return and report for duty on Thursday.

Forty members of Clarendon Press, Oxford, returned. L.N.E.R. announce 1,000 trains working.

'LEGALITY NO QUIBBLE.'

Employees of the Star Process Engraving Co., Ltd., Manchester, on May 6, refused to obey what they called the 'illegal demand' of their union that they cease work. They claimed right, nevertheless, to continue membership and receive full benefits. Branch Secretary replied that this was 'quibble' and 'defiance.' Employees stood pat, quoting Sir John Simon and Government guarantee.

STRIKE ITEMS.

All companies announced for Manchester theatres arrived by road or rail.

Chancery Division judge refused committal orders against judgment debtors who failed answer summonses. 300 students left Cambridge assist unloading ships at Hull. Two fish trains, one for

Manchester and one for London, left Grimsby. Twenty per cent Huddersfield trams, running. Sixty-one Leeds trams running. Writ Hammersmith North by-election postponed.

Government reported to have commandeered Argus Press printing works, London. All leading London stores report serious fall in trade. Over 400 independent 'buses running in London. Boulogne telegram says vegetable cargoes rotting in British ships thrown overboard.

Not a single Bradford textile mill closed, but 13,000 on short time. Leicester staple industries hard hit and 14,000 idle. Torquay unaffected, except for idleness of 1,100 builders. Preston transport difficulties smoothed out. Sixteen vessels docked and undocked at Liverpool yesterday. Popular public houses closed through lack of supplies. Yorkshire miners (150,000) to receive strike pay on Thursday (men 20/-; boys up to 18/-; 2/- per child).

Thirty Hull rioters sentenced 3 and 6 months. Three Fulham men 21 days for circulating pamphlet alleging Welsh Guards mutiny. Four Chelsea men sentenced for assault on police. 'Dirty and cowardly,' said Thames magistrate sentencing one of crowd who threw bottles and glasses at single policeman. Croydon platelayer two months for threatening volunteers with hammer. Three months for Southwark man who threw brick at police.

More than a million passengers carried by Metropolitan Railway since strike. Soup kitchen for poor children opening in East Fulham by local Conservative Association (women's branch).

A.B.C. cafe drivers struck yesterday, but when Ministry of Transport supplied 60 volunteers number of strikers returned. Two Huddersfield 'bus drivers injured by rowdies. Norwich strike committee, in conjunction with chief constable, arranging athletic meetings. Students drove corporation 'buses yesterday at Aberdeen, where all was quiet.

Annual Meeting will be held of Manchester Warehousemen and Clerks' Orphan Schools, 80, Mosley-street, Manchester, May 19th, 1-30 p.m. Election of children as usual.

GUARANTEE TO WORKERS.
Legislation Likely.

(From our Political Correspondent.)

London, Monday.

I understand that Government's view is that it may be advisable to confirm by legislation assurances given to men remaining at work or returning to work that they shall not be victimised by deprivation of pensions or other benefits. It is admitted that Sir J. Simon is right, but to make it clear and simple what would amount to a declaratory Act may be passed. I am assured authoritatively, however, that Government has no intention of tampering with general trade union law. Anything that it is considering is in nature of special questions arising out of what is, in fact, an illegal strike in breach of contracts.

The Government is aware that one thing that is influencing moderates in Labour party and trade union movement is feeling that they must fight this struggle out and win it, because if they do not win whole of trade unionism would go. It is, therefore, desired to make it clear that Government has nothing of that kind in mind.

STRIKERS' FUNDS FROM ABROAD.

GERMAN SUBSCRIPTION LIST.

(From our Berlin Correspondent.)

Subscription lists distributed to all trade union branch offices here. All who wish to contribute to funds of British unions during strike are asked to enter names on these lists. Expected that response will be very big all over Germany, and that even non-union labour will participate.

£5,000 FROM HOLLAND.

International Federation of Trade Unions, Amsterdam, has sent letter to all centres asking them immediately to open relief funds, and remit money to General Council direct. Dutch Federation has sent first contribution of £5,000.

TRANS-ATLANTIC HELP.

Sydney (Nova Scotia) District Union of coal miners will co-operate with British strikers and oppose shipment to Great Britain.

All-India Trade Union Congress has cabled further sum of £300 in addition to £200 cabled on Friday to T.U.C.

NO SYMPATHY STRIKE ON CONTINENT.

Mr. Frank Hodges, secretary Miners' International, says no request for general strike on Continent; question not considered at Ostend. Resolution passed bans export of coal to Britain, and proposes financial aid for British miners.

THE FLOUR CONVOYS.

Central Food Committee states:— 'Rail supplies for Hyde Park milk pool coming so freely that lorries released for other urgent services. Convoy of 220 lorries with flour from Victoria Docks to Hyde Park yesterday with escort of armoured cars, troops and police. London flour supplies now fully secured.'

G.W.R. ran 500 trains on Sunday and 600 yesterday. L.M.S. ran 1,000 yesterday; L.N.E.R. 1,000.

Between Gosforth and Newcastle yesterday 50 men stoned passing motor cars and overturned lorry with salmon from Berwick. Police arrived and made several arrests.

MANCHESTER.

STRIKE IN FLOUR MILLS.

Manchester tramways, inviting men to report for duty to-morrow morning. Number of Salford tramwaymen presented themselves for duty yesterday; volunteer drivers also enrolled. Possible attempt to run a skeleton service to-day. E.T.U. threaten if trams run in Manchester or Salford electric power stops. Some hundred men in Manchester and Salford flour mills struck. C.W.S. mills working. Manchester picket sentenced to two months for interfering with load of flour in Hulme.

Manchester Tramways Committee's invitation to men is: Committee intimate to men that they are public servants and their action in declining to operate public tramways is causing inconvenience to public. Committee therefore request that those of their employees who are desirous of continuing in the public service and are willing to report for duty should do so to the various sheds on Wednesday morning next.

Emergency Committee state that though strike at flour mills yesterday affected all mills but one in Manchester district, food supplies are being satisfactorily maintained and there is no fear of shortage. The employees at the remaining mill (C.W.S. Sun) decided not to work to-day. Number of volunteers offering services in Manchester yesterday surpassed all previous days. Committee add that supplies of fish are good. Provisions coming through satisfactorily.

Governors of Manchester High School yesterday decided to make no change in Whitsuntide holiday dates; school carries on as arranged.

BRISTOL MILLERS VOTE AGAINST STRIKE.

Employees at Spillers' & Baker's flour mills, Bristol, decided yesterday by 102 votes against 13 to remain at work.

GLASGOW QUIET.

(From our Special Correspondent.)

Glasgow, Monday.

Quiet since Saturday night. Police vigour produced healthy impression on turbulent elements. About 250 arrested to date. Transport services improving; 300 trams running, manned chiefly by University students, but regular men returning, including 60 to-day. Eight vessels unloading under protected ratings from warships Hood, Warspite and Comus now in Clyde. Provisions being sent Western Isles, where shortage flour reported. Subway line reopened to-day.

CADIFF TRAM STRIKE COLLAPSES.

(From our special correspondents)

Cardiff, Monday.

Cardiff in particular, and South Wales in general, still more peaceful; no industrial district can have cleaner record. Not an abnormal incident to-day. Most notable happening collapse of tram strike. Men told to-day to return within 24 hours, or consider themselves discharged; 114 back, and repair staff returning to-morrow.

STOPPAGE OF FOOD FROM IRELAND.
Labour Request.

(From our Labour Correspondent.)

London, Monday.

General Council would not say to-day whether it is correct that embargo has been placed, at its request, on export of goods, including foodstuffs, from Ireland. Such request has, however, been made, and Dublin dockers have acted on it. Belfast dockers will not handle cargoes after Wednesday.

British Gazette this morning gives coloured and misleading account of meetings of miners' and transport workers' Internationals at Ostend. Question of international coal strike not considered. Meeting declared an embargo on coal exports to England and bunkering of British ships, and in favour of levies on members to support British miners. Miners in Ruhr and Czechoslovakia have made similar declarations.

There have been rumours to-day of informal discussion between the Government and representatives of the T.U.C. There is no truth in them.

Announced to-night that Electrical Trades Union has decided that in future all permits for electricity must be issued through T.U.C. General Council in London.

HOUSE OF COMMONS.

CHARGE AGAINST POLICE DENIED.

SUPPRESSION OF ARCHBISHOP'S MESSAGE.

Mr. Lloyd George asked in Commons yesterday why 'British Gazette' suppressed appeal of church leaders issued by Archbishop. Dispute could not be settled except on some such terms without incalculable disaster. Bad policy to talk of breaking strikers. This remark led to uproar on the Government benches. Mr. Churchill said under difficulties of producing paper, impossible to avoid many mistakes, omission and commission. Promised to publish article soon as possible, but it would be better if T.U.C. allowed papers to publish.

Dr. Haden Guest alleged that on Friday night lorry load of police entered Southwark public house, beat customers over heads and bodies with truncheons before they had time to leave seats. Men, he further alleged, were bludgeoned as they ran into the street. Police proceeded to raid district, using abusive and obscene language, chased women and charged crowd of children. Broke open door of house. People near Elephant and Castle burned 'bus, and afterwards district was raided by police and people terrified. Home Secretary replied that Southwark was a lively district. There had been much disorder there, and the Mayor had to appeal for police protection to take coal to houses where there was illness. Police account of incident mentioned by Dr. Guest was that men in public house had assaulted special, and they were turned out; police cleared streets. No women or children interfered with. There was no undue assault on anybody. After full consideration he found the police had not exceeded duties.

Mr. Charleton (Labour, Leeds) described specials as blackguardly hooligans. He saw mounted policeman deliberately ride horse on pavement against shoppers, and after 'bus incident specials truncheoned men, women and children.

Other Labour members condemned unnecessary use of specials and Tory members protested against 'unfounded charges' against police calculated to prejudice public. Supporting Mr. George's protest Mr. Ammon said that but for suppression of Archbishop's appeal we might now be discussing terms of peace.

Sir H. Slesser challenged Sir J. Simon's statement of strike law. Attorney General said his view was courts would restrain any attempt to penalise trade unionists for disobeying illegal order.

The debate on the Home Office vote was adjourned, and the House rose at 8-45.

Two men given lift by motorist in Manchester thanked him as they got out, and added: 'We are just going on picket duty.'

Two men buried while mining outcrop seam near Wigan.

PERSONAL MEDIATION.
Sir H. Samuel in Touch with Both Sides.

(From our Political Correspondent.)

London, Monday.

Sir Herbert Samuel has been in touch to-day both with the miners and with the mineowners. I do not say that he has seen either. His action is, formally at any rate, entirely on his own initiative and responsibility.

It would be idle to deny that Government is watching with interest. If the miners and the owners were to agree under Sir Herbert Samuel's persuasion, the whole strike would end naturally.

GOVERNMENT OUTLOOK.

An Official statement issued yesterday evening says: Arrangements for distribution of milk, food and petrol supplies more successful than on any other day of strike. Unloading and transportation of commodities is approaching normality. Emergency arrangements of Government are working thoroughly. In particular, the situation at the London docks and at other parts is well in hand. Supply of light and power continues remarkably satisfactory, while railway services show progressive improvement. One-fifth of the regular staffs of the railway companies are at work, and there is an abundant supply of volunteers to take the place of those on strike. Nearly four thousand trains will be run to-day.

PLEA FOR TAXPAYER.

Mr. F.W. Hirst, formerly Editor of the Economist, writes to us: 'The impasse, as you say, is deplorable. The taxpayer has a right to be heard. A perfectly simple solution is available. Let the coalowners open or reopen all the mines which can be opened without loss, and let the sympathetic strike, which must be costing the country in Government expenditure and business losses a million a day, and perhaps more, be called off simultaneously. If something is not done, and quickly, we shall be faced with another crushing increase of taxation owing to a reduced public revenue and a heavily increased public expenditure. Hundreds of business men are being ruined, and thousands of people, perhaps tens of thousands, or even hundreds of thousands, will be thrown on the dole or the rates.

MR. MACDONALD.

Mr. J. Ramsay Macdonald writes to the *British Independent*:– "This dispute ought never to have happened and had the problems in dispute been handled with ordinary care and common sense there would have been neither lock-out nor strike. On one thing I can give the nation the most confident assurance. The general strike in support of the miners was never meant as, and even now it is not, a strike against Parliament, the Government, or the Constitution. For purely war propaganda purposes the Government says it is. Good will and calm heads will in the end prevail. We are working literally night and day that that may be soon.

Leader   # THE TRUE TEMPER.

Mr. Lloyd George did a public service yesterday when he called attention to the omission from the 'British Gazette,' the official paper published by the government, of any mention of the very important manifesto issued late on Friday by the Archbishop of Canterbury and a number of the Free Church leaders proposing the terms of a settlement of the industrial war. This manifesto, which appeared in a portion of our Thursday's issue and was repeated in Monday's, called for cancellation of the strike, withdrawal of the mineowners' notices and a brief extension of the subsidy. It was a wise pronouncement worthy of its authors. It was unfortunately not seen as worthy of the columns of the official 'Gazette.' For this Mr. Churchill made some lame excuses yesterday coupled with an impertinent rebuke to Mr. Lloyd George venturing to expose his own short-coming. To the demand that the manifesto should be printed to-morrow he appears to have given an evasive reply. The manifesto is, of course, in direct opposition to the policy of 'Gazette' as directed by Mr. Churchill. That is reason the more why it should have been and should be published if the 'Gazette' is not to be regarded as a partisan publication. Happily the Archbishop's sermon broadcasted on Sunday drives its version home. It is by this temper and this temper alone that the nation can be saved from immeasurable calamities.

Leader **IS IT AN INDUSTRIAL STRIKE?**

The Manchester Tramways Committee is making an appeal to its employees. It is reminding them that the trams are a public service, run for the convenience of the public. It is asking those of its employees who wish to remain in its service to report for duty on Wednesday. In this way is raised an issue which lies at the root of the whole strike policy. The Trade Unions Council last week formally and emphatically declared that the general strike was purely industrial and that no constitutional issue was raised by it. Why, then, are the tramway employees on strike? They have no grievance against their employers. It is the public who both own and use the trams. Is not the conclusion inevitable that the tramwaymen have been called out because their absence will inconvenience the public and so add to the general public confusion and loss? Have not all the trade unionists who have been called out been selected just because they were the men whose absence could be most keenly felt by the public? Is not that why they were called 'the first line troops'?

The tramwaymen are under no legal or moral obligation to obey the illegal instructions of the Trade Unions Council. On the contrary they are under a legal and moral obligation to the public. It is a perverted and almost incomprehensible sense of loyalty which now keeps them from work and which demands almost intolerable sacrifices from them as well as from the public. In their interests as well as in those of the rest of us let us hope that Wednesday will see the beginning of a return to sanity and of the refutation of the vicious principle that the public, through its representative institutions, can be coerced by a section of the community.

TRAIN ACCIDENTS.
Four Passengers Killed.

The 1.6 p.m. train from Berwick to Edinburgh ran into some goods wagons at St. Margarets; three passengers killed and several injured. The 10 o'clock from Edinburgh to King's Cross had mishap near Newcastle; engine and several coaches derailed but only one passenger hurt and train men escaped. Man killed and another injured in collision between passenger and goods trains in Bishops Stortford station.

Northumberland smash believed caused by foul play; a fish plate removed. Train carried 500 passengers and was worked by 5 volunteers. In Edinburgh accident, 6 passengers, police and rescuers gassed by fumes in tunnel, where smash occurred.

On Wednesday May 12 the 'Guardian' was able to increase its size substantially and produce a four-page edition.

Wednesday May 12 1926   *p.3*

ON THE EVE OF STRIKE DEVELOPMENTS.
T.U.C. Calls Out the Engineers

IMPORTANT DISCUSSIONS AT LABOUR HEADQUARTERS.
Liberal Peace Move.

HIGH COURT DECISION DECLARES THE STRIKE ILLEGAL.

The opening of the second week of the general strike was marked by important developments.

The T.U.C. and the miners' leaders held long meetings, and last night T.U.C. General Council held specially summoned meeting, which Mr. Thomas attended, 'in order to open door if possible or keep it open for resumed negotiations.' Later, there was a joint meeting of the T.U.C. and miners, and discussions were likely to be continued late into the night.

Meanwhile, T.U.C. orders to engineers and shipyard workers to cease work this morning, as 'the second line,' had been received all over the country. Reports from various centres suggested that there was some division of opinion as to obeying this order. In Manchester the shops are being kept open for those men who stay at work.

A peace move was initiated in the House of Commons last night by Sir John Simon, speaking for the whole Parliamentary Liberal party. To-day he is tabling a motion calling for a Government offer of assistance to the coal industry for a short period, conditional upon the calling off of the general strike and undertakings by owners and miners.

In the High Court, Mr. Justice Astbury gave a very important decision declaring the general strike to be illegal, and defining the position in regard to use of union funds for strike pay.

STRIKE LEADERS IN COUNCIL.

(From our Labour Correspondent.)

London, Tuesday.

The soundings and informal discussions of the last two days bore fruit to-day, when the General Council and the Miners' Executive discussed their position. The Miners' Executive met at Russell Square, and Mr. Ramsay MacDonald called there before he went on to Eccleston Square, where the General Council was meeting. The miners sat all morning and afternoon, and at the close of their meeting Mr. A.J. Cook made the following statement:

The Miners' Federation Executive met this morning and reviewed the position in the light of messages received from all over the coalfields appealing to the Executive to stand firm against any compromise on either hours, wages, or national agreements.

On behalf of the Executive I desire to inform the miners and the general public that we are as firm to-day as we were when the miners decided unanimously, after the question had been referred to every district, that there were to be no reductions in wages. In the words of our president, Mr. Herbert Smith, 'We have nowt to give.' There have been no negotiations (Mr. Cook continued in reply to a question). There are many influences, I understand, at work with the object of finding a bridge, but whatever bridge is found it must be one that will ensure the status quo at least for the miners.

The General Council met again at six o'clock, and the Miners' Executive joined them at eight o'clock. They were meeting Mr. Poulton, the General Council's spokesman said 'further to explore the position, because we don't want to leave any door shut if we feel we can keep it open.'

11 p.m.

The two bodies consulted on the basis on which they will be prepared to negotiate when the point of negotiations is reached. The unofficial peace efforts have been directed to discovering a formula on which the coal negotiations can proceed and the means by which the proposals of the Report are to be considered by all parties.

Mr. Cook's statement to-day is the purely official view and must be read as repeating that publicly the Executive has not power to go beyond its earlier instructions. It does not mean that the miners will not discuss things in a different spirit in private negotiations, but in view of their delegate conference decisions and the firmness of the men in the coalfields they cannot move on quickly as most earnest outside peacemakers would like them to do. The same thing in a rather different way, of course, could be said of the Government.

SIR J. SIMON'S PLAN.

Government and Discussions Behind the Scenes.

(From our Political Correspondent.)

London, Tuesday Night.

Sir John Simon's proposal for a settlement of the strike in the House of Commons debate to-day represents the view of the whole of the Liberal Parliamentary party. To-morrow he will table a motion, which he will ask the Government to announce its willingness for a short period to give assistance to the coal industry on the understanding that the following conditions are satisfied concurrently:–

(1) The immediate and unqualified calling off of the general strike.

(2) That there should be a reopening of the mines by the coalowners at the old rates from day to day.

(3) The Government to prepare legislation to carry out the recommendations of the Commission.

(4) That those who speak for the miners on the one hand and the coalowners on the other should give a definite undertaking that they will forthwith negotiate on the basis of the contents of the report, without excluding from it anything which it contains.

On the Government's side the comment is that somewhere along those lines the solution will probably have to come, but the difficulty is in the word 'concurrently.' The Government so far holds to its condition that the general strike must be called off first before there can be any discussion at all.

Mr. Justice Astbury's decision that the general strike as distinct from the miners' strike is not a trade dispute within the meaning of the Act represents the view of the Government, but even if the decision be upheld in the highest court it does not follow that legislation would be regarded as unnecessary. The law officers of the Crown have been considering the legal position for some time.

As far as the judgment is concerned, the Attorney General and the Home Secretary have no locus standi. It would be a matter of actions by individual trade unionists and individual firms. The Government's guarantee against victimisation and the forfeiting of benefits will probably be fulfilled by legislation.

Conversations in Progress

There was a very long Cabinet meeting at six o'clock this evening. It lasted over an hour and a half. One is assured, however, that there is nothing in the way of negotiation going on behind the scenes, and that the Government has taken no part in negotiations of any kind, formal or informal. This may be so, but conversations of importance are going on and it is difficult to believe that the Government is not cognisant of them or is entirely indifferent to them.

The real focus of the negotiations in this period was the discussion being held between the TUC and Sir Herbert Samuel. For further details of Mr. Justice Astbury's decision, see the 'Chronology of Main Events'.

p.2

OUR LONDON CORRESPONDENCE

By Private Wire.

London, Tuesday Night.

A BRIGHTER GLIMPSE.

Although there was little definite news to account for it, and Mr. Cook's statement in the evening damped it all again, there was a noticeable brightening to-day of the general outlook. Possibly it spread from the City, where movements in War Loan and the dollar exchange gave real cause of satisfaction. But behind it all was the feeling that things could not go on, and that the trade union leaders are striving to get back to the position on Sunday night, and that Mr. Baldwin could be expected to hold down his die-hards in the end.

The last two days have been remarkably peaceful in London, and even the unloading of paper for the 'British Gazette' in its quarters next door to the almost paperless 'British Worker' did not rouse any disturbance. Transport is much easier, and sometimes five 'buses are to be seen together.

The food situation is hardly changed, and the only shortage is in Poplar and one or two other districts where there is no beer. Some breweries will not now deliver, and the publicans are arranging to collect themselves or do without. On the other hand, cats-meat is regularly being delivered.

MR. COOK'S STATEMENT.

Mr. Cook's statement to-day has caused disappointment and concern among those who were hoping for peace and seeking means of obtaining it. If the miners are not ready now even to consider the part of the Report relating to the wages question they have actually receded from their position in the concluding stage of negotiations.

With the shadow of catastrophe hanging over the whole world of labour no set of men are justified in pressing such a claim, whatever its cost to their fellow-workers and to the fortunes both of the trade unions and of the Labour movement. If this attitude is maintained it will make very much more difficult the already tremendous task of the peacemakers inside as well as outside the trade unions.

NEWSPAPERS.

To-day the 'Daily Chronicle' appeared, the first Liberal paper published in London during the strike. It has four small pages, and gives prominence to the Archbishop's appeal, supporting it as the basis for peace. The 'British Independent,' a non-party daily of five typed sheets, working for conciliation and run by Oxford undergraduates, is also out.

There is much comment on the splendid stand for a humane settlement made by three institutions that the public does not always associate with running against middle-class sentiment – the Church, Oxford, and Cambridge; although it must be added that the Cambridge die-hards, too, have had their say.

Papers from Yorkshire, Sheffield, Plymouth, and Bristol are selling in the streets, as well as some London papers. The 'British Worker,' now of a very small size owing to shortage of paper, is issued in the evening. The 'British Gazette' is now being printed in Tudor Street, next door to the 'Daily Herald,' as well as in the 'Morning Post' office. Many shops are now posting newspapers in their windows, and some taverns and teashops are now keeping a newspaper for general use, as in Regency days.

THREE-PARTY BROADCASTING CLAIM.

I understand that a suggestion has been made to Mr. J.C.C. Davidson, Financial Secretary to the Admiralty, who is looking after the broadcasting policy for the Government, that the Parliamentary report on the wireless should be a report drawn up by agreement between the Whips of the three parties. I understand that nothing of the kind has yet been arranged, and that practical difficulties in the way of it are admitted on all sides. It ought not to be past the wit of the government to broadcast a fair report. Any independent newspaper or competent journalist could show it the way.

Meanwhile I understand that Mr. Ramsay MacDonald has applied for permission to broadcast, and that there was a very long sitting of the Governmental authority in charge, which eventually adjourned until six o'clock to-day, to give its decision. To make the permission a more practical thing I understand that Mr. Lloyd George has also applied, so that there is now an application filed by each of the Opposition leaders and ex-Prime Ministers in the House of Commons.

A VOLUNTARY SUBSIDY?

'A Woman Teacher' writes:– Has it ever been suggested that a voluntary subsidy should be given to the miners until there has been time to place the coal industry on a better footing? I am a woman teacher in a small way, but I would willingly give towards it, and there must be many thousands of other people who could and would do far more if it would help to stop the strike. Is this practicable?

p.3

ABSENCE OF DISORDER
Cheerful Tone of Government Report

(From our London Staff.)

Fleet-street, Tuesday night.

The interesting thing about the information supplied by a Government official to the journalists to-night was its unsensational character. The only disorder of any importance announced was a 'highly organised' attempt to stop the 'buses at Blaydon and Chopwell, in County Durham, by 'gangs of roughs,' and this happened on Saturday. As a result of this affair two arrests have been made under Section 21 of the Emergency Regulations, that is, on a charge of sedition. A cheerful report was given of conditions generally so far as the absence of disorder and the maintenance of the essential services are concerned. In the northern division, for example, 'the conditions generally have improved, and there is an increasing spirit of confidence throughout.'

Returning to Work.
The other interesting feature of this official summary was the

news of men returning to work in a few districts. All the workers at a flour mill at Maidstone, 'owing to the possibility of being called upon to strike and with a view of showing their loyalty to the country, have seceded from their union,' and a large proportion of strikers at mills at Deptford and Greenwich have gone back. The employees at the Bedford Electricity Department have signed an undertaking to return and remain at work and not to terminate their engagement in the future without giving proper notice. Some employees at the Unic Works have returned.

Smithfield Market is now a 'protected area,' i.e., it is enclosed in barriers and the workers are assured of full protection.

p.3

CITY'S FOOD SUPPLIES.

Careful arrangements have been made in Manchester to ensure that there is no lack of flour in the city. It is understood that there is no danger of a shortage on this or any other foodstuffs. With the help of the volunteers who took up quarters in the docks yesterday the Committee anticipate that they will find no difficulty in resuming the delivery of grain to the flour mills. Even should the supply of flour from outside towns such as Liverpool be curtailed, it is expected that it will be possible to supply the city from mills run by volunteers. Increased supplies of foodstuffs are arriving by rail. No real transport difficulty has been experienced in Manchester, and a satisfactory measure of good feeling has existed between pickets and drivers of vans and lorries.

The official statement which was made yesterday by the Emergency Committee expresses satisfaction at the transport of foodstuffs and the ability of its services to meet all demands, and points out that a particular wholesaler who has increased the price of potatoes 50 per cent may be forced by the Civil Commissioner to accept control of his prices.

SPECIAL CONSTABLES ATTACKED.

Twenty-seven special constables on their way to Birkenhead police office yesterday were attacked by hooligans. Four were hurt, one being taken to hospital. Police were rushed to the scene in charabancs.

MOTOR LORRY FIRED
Attack on Volunteer Transport.

Prosecuted under the Emergency Powers Act at Manchester City Police Court yesterday for inciting a crowd of people to set fire to a motor-lorry manned by volunteers in Piccadilly, Manchester, on Tuesday night, Peter Tilley (36), of Clements Street, Higher Openshaw; John Marshall (57), of Stanton Street, Openshaw; and John Marsland (27), of Brideoak Street, Hightown, were each sentenced to three months' imprisonment with hard labour. All three men denied the charges.

Mr. Fred Webster, of the Town Clerk's Department, prosecuting, said this was the most serious case that had occurred in the city in connection with the strike. The accused were in the forefront of a crowd of people shouting 'Burn the — lorry!' 'Turn it over!' 'Stop the — blacklegs!' It was alleged that they climbed on the bonnet of a motor-lorry belonging to the London Midland and Scottish Railway while in transit from London Road Station to Victoria Station, Manchester, conveying eggs, butter, bicycles, and parcels. The motor-lorry was partly destroyed. The accused men climbed on the bonnet of the motor-lorry and attempted to interfere with the machinery of the vehicle. The bonnet of the car was torn off, the petrol pipe broken, and lighted matches were thrown by someone into its engine. The foodstuffs and other articles were rendered useless.

An Irresponsible Mischief-Maker.

Under the Emergency Powers Act, Thomas Smith (46) of Slater Street, Oldham Road, Manchester, was charged at Manchester City Police Court yesterday with 'committing an act likely to cause disaffection among the civilian population,' and was sentenced by the Stipendiary Magistrate (Mr. E. Brierley) to one month's imprisonment.

Mr. Fred Webster, senior assistant solicitor in the Town Clerk's Department, prosecuting, said Smith went ahead of the usual rent collector to houses in Slater Street, and when the doors were opened he shouted to the tenant, 'Don't pay the rent!' In other cases he handed them slips of paper, on which was written in pencil: 'T.U.C. Don't pay your rent. While you pay your rent you help the Government.'

Answering the Stipendiary Magistrate, Smith, who admitted the offence, said it was 'a drunken freak' on his part. He had no connection with the T.U.C. and was not a member of any trade union.

POLICE RAID STRIKE CENTRE.
Local Leaders Charged.

The B.B.C. last evening announced that following a police raid on Tuesday night at the offices of the Birmingham Joint Trade Union Emergency Committee, which has been publishing a daily strike bulletin, some twenty leading Labour representatives, supposed to have been engaged in the production, were charged with publishing a false statement likely to cause disaffection. The defendants, who include some local Labour magistrates, were remanded on bail.

RED HANDS BEHIND THE STRIKE.
Home Office Proofs.

(From our own Correspondent.)

Paris, Tuesday.

Word has been given to all the French journalists in London that the Home Office has 'proofs' of a sinister long-planned Russian plot of which the general strike is the outcome. No charge is made against the trade union leaders of being conscious accomplices; on the contrary, they are represented as innocent tools in the hands of these Red plotters, who number only some hundreds. They were directed formerly from the Russian Embassy in London, now from the Paris Embassy, and have long foreseen and worked for this catastrophe. French pressmen are mainly incredulous of this fantastic nonsense.

According to 'Pertinax,' Sir William Joynson-Hicks has a tremendous police dossier upon this Red plot and will communicate it to Parliament. 'Pertinax' is told that a prominent member of the Trade Unions Congress has recently been in Paris to consult Mr. Rakovsky, the Soviet Charge d'Affaires.

CALLING OUT THE ENGINEERS.
Secret T.U.C. Orders.

TO CEASE WORK LAST NIGHT.

(From our Labour Correspondent.)

London, Tuesday.

The General Council has issued secret instructions to the engineering and shipbuilding unions that their members must cease work to-night. The original decision applied only to the iron and steel workers and certain classes of engineers engaged on maintenance work. The General Council has consistently denied that the 'secondline' has been called out by national action, and it was stated this morning that any such action 'is being initiated locally without any direct instructions from the T.U.C.'

There is, however, good reason for saying that the instruction to the engineers and shipyard workers was addressed yesterday from Eccleston Square, and this is confirmed by reports to-day from all the chief centres. So far it appears that the dockyards and Government undertakings are not affected. Many of the unions are taking action, and the response will be an important test of the vitality of the strike and of the influence on the men of the Government's assurances of protection.

The secret instructions sent to the unions are as follows:– 'The Trade Union Congress Strike Organisation Committee has decided that the Engineering and Shipbuilding Trades shall, unless otherwise ordered, refrain from starting work on Wednesday, May 12. This applies to all unions. This order does not apply to men engaged in H.M. Dockyards, Admiralty shipyards, and Government engineering establishments.'

At Birkenhead the following notice has been posted:– 'In accordance with instructions received from the T.U.C. General Council the Merseyside Council of Action hereby orders all workers engaged in shipyards and dockyards to cease work at 5 p.m., Tuesday, May 11. This order to apply to all workmen.'

The Amalgamated Engineering Union has sent out a similar order, saying: 'The Executive Council requests all members to give effect to the General Council's instructions.'

CENTRES.

Reports from some centres last night showed that the order was being obeyed, but there were indications of divisions at a number of others.

Our South Shields correspondent telegraphs: Many shipyard workers are opposed to strike action, and resolutions have been passed to-day at some yards deciding not to come out. It is believed that the response to the strike call will prove a fiasco so far as the yards on the lower Tyne are concerned.

Boilermakers and shipwrights at Palmer's Yard, Jarrow, resolved to continue working.

Shipyard workers at Smith's Docks, Middlesbrough, declined to come out on strike until a national ballot was taken.

Some trades in the Tyne shipyards decided to leave work; others, including the boilermakers and shipwrights, refused.

Clyde engineers and shipyard workers are reported divided. It is stated that the boilermakers have been notified that individuals leave work on their responsibility as no ballot has been taken.

By 189 votes to 146 A.E.U. members at Rushton and Hornsby's, Grantham, decided to obey.

SITUATION ON CLYDE.

Engineers Called Out.

(From our Special Correspondent.)

Glasgow, Tuesday.

According to the 'Scottish Worker,' the official organ of the Scottish Trade Unions Congress, the engineering and shipbuilding trade unions have arranged for their employed members to cease work at 5.30 to-night in accordance with the instructions of the General Council of the Trade Unions Congress.

This means, says the newspaper quoted, that all the Clyde shipyards and engineering shops will close down, and that about 80,000 more Clyde men will join the strike.

The shipbuilding and engineering trades in Dundee, Aberdeen, Leith, Burntisland, and elsewhere in the East of Scotland are also expected to stop work to-night, so that 100,000 Scottish artisans are expected to answer the latest call of the T.U.C. General Council.

The city tram service has improved considerably to-day. Many more men are reported to have returned to work, and more than half the usual number of cars are now in the streets. Superficial observation suggests that the tram strike is rapidly approaching the point of collapse. Services on the Subway are to be extended to-morrow.

A new form of picketing is reported from the southern side of the city. Women wearing red rosettes are standing at the stopping places on the car routes and endeavouring to persuade members of the public not to use the cars.

One woman picket appeared at one of the City Police Courts this morning charged with creating a disturbance, inciting to violence, and assaulting a conductor.

p.2

THE ARCHBISHOP'S CALL
Full Text.

We publish to-day the full text of the churches' concordat appeal issued by the Archbishop of Canterbury, summaries of which have already appeared in our emergency editions. The appeal was sent to the British Broadcasting Company for broadcasting and to the official Government paper on Friday night last. It was published yesterday by the B.B.C. following protests against its non-publication in the 'British Gazette' made in the House of Commons by Mr. Lloyd George and others. The text is as follows:–

Representatives of the Christian churches in England are convinced that a real settlement will only be achieved in a spirit of fellowship and co-operation for the common good, and not as a result of war.

Realising that the longer the present struggle persists the greater will be the suffering and loss, they earnestly request that all the parties concerned in this dispute will agree to resume negotiations undeterred by obstacles which have been created by the events of the last few days.

If it should seem to be incumbent on us to suggest a definite line of approach, we would submit, as the basis of a possible concordat, a return to the *status quo* of Friday week. We cannot but believe in the possibility of a successful issue. Our proposal should be interpreted as involving simultaneously and concurrently–

(1) The cancellation on the part of the T.U.C. of the general strike.

(2) Renewal by the Government of its offer of assistance to the coal industry for a short definite period.

(3) The withdrawal on the part of the mineowners of the new wages scales recently issued.

We understand that the Archbishop's appeal is appearing in to-day's 'British Gazette' printed last night.

CANADIAN CONTRIBUTION.

(Reuter's Telegram.)

Ottawa, Tuesday.

The first Canadian contribution of £100 for the British Trade Union Congress strike fund has been forwarded by the Canadian Brotherhood of Railway Employees, to be used as the General Council sees fit.

Mr. P.M. Draper, the secretary of the Canadian Trades Labour Congress, sent out a series of telegrams last night to the district councils of organised labour in Canada asking them to forward immediately to Ottawa, for transmission to the British strike fund, monetary contributions 'to assist organised labour in Great Britain in the present crisis.'

Leader
ILLEGAL STRIKES.

The public in general, and employers of labour in particular, have lived for so long under the threat of the lightning strike that is was quite generally assumed that in such cases the law was a formal abstraction which could be ignored at will, and of which the breach entailed no penalties. Immunity arose, among other things, from the fact that the number of men engaged in an illegal dispute was commonly too large to be prosecuted, and that disputes cannot usually be ended unless there is a complete amnesty. No alteration in the law can affect those facts. Nevertheless the law is not entirely impotent, and when the whole nation is threatened by its defiance may be invoked with unexpected effect. The first inkling of the legal implications of the present strike was given by Sir John Simon in the House of Commons last week. His warning that members of trade unions who refused to obey an unlawful instruction to strike could not be deprived of their benefit ought to have been common knowledge. In fact, it fell like a bombshell. It is now supplemented by a legal decision which carries the consequences of taking part in an illegal strike a good deal further. In granting an injunction to restrain certain officers of the National Sailors and Firemen's Union from calling their members out on strike contrary to the rules of their union Mr. Justice Astbury made some comments which were of more general application.

Sir John Simon had dealt with the illegality of striking without giving the proper notice, that is of the lightning strike. Mr. Justice

Astbury went further and declared that the general strike was in itself illegal. It would, if we understand him correctly, have been equally illegal if formal notice had been given. 'No trade dispute,' he said, 'has been alleged or shown to exist in any of the unions affected, except in the miners' case, and no trade dispute does or can exist between the Trade Unions Congress on the one hand and the Government and the nation on the other.' Not merely, therefore, is the general strike unlawful, but it is not even a strike in furtherance of a trade dispute, and those persons, according to Mr. Justice Astbury, who take part in it 'are not protected by the Trade Disputes Act of 1906.' This is the Act which gives immunity at law to all members of a trade union 'in respect of any tortuous act alleged to have been committed by or on behalf of the trade union.' The wisdom of this provision in the Trade Disputes Act has been often challenged. But the question of its wisdom does not now arise. What does arise is the fact that, as stated by Mr. Justice Astbury, trade unions are debarred not only from withholding benefits from members who disobey its illegal instructions but also from paying strike pay to those who do, and that they cannot rely upon the shelter of the Trade Disputes Act for protection.

What is the effect? At the first blush it might seem as though trade unionism were being attacked and its foundations undermined by a series of unexpected legal pronouncements. Nothing could be more untrue. Trade unionism and the rights of the trade unions stand exactly where they were. It is only the enlargement of the trade union idea far beyond its original and legitimate scope that is affected, and there are thousands of the most loyal trade unionists who, so far from being alarmed, will rejoice at the fact. Mr. Thomas openly and courageously declared the other day that he was opposed to the whole conception of the general strike, and when, after inflicting enormous loss alike on its supporters and its opponents, it has failed, as it will fail, there will be multitudes who will agree with him. Attempts no doubt will be made by irresponsible people to make the general strike a pretext for an attack upon the trade unions, and a preposterous demand was actually put forward yesterday by the 'Daily Mail' for the suppression of the Trade Unions Council. It is quite sufficient that its present policy should fail and that in the prosecution of that policy the law should have struck its chief weapons from its hands. But the whole edifice of trade unionism, as protected by law and approved by public opinion, stands and will stand. Mr. Baldwin has already declared that he will be no party to an attack upon it.

Leader   **FOOD SUPPLIES.**

The ordinary housekeeper would have no reason to imagine that a general strike had been proclaimed, and to a large extent enforced, over a week ago. It is reflected neither in the price nor in the quantity of the food supplies of the shops. For this satisfactory state of affairs there does not appear to be much gratitude owing to the Trade Unions Council. The Council, it is true, originally offered to run some kind of food service, but the Government obviously could not permit the country to be rationed by the kindness and at the discretion of the T.U.C. After that local arrangements appear to have been generally made for the issue of permits and for distribution of supplies by agreement with the unions. These arrangements seem to have come to an end in most places, either because the permits were abused or because the trade unions had changed their policy. What their policy is now it is their duty to state. The 'British Worker' said yesterday that the T.U.C. had done 'nothing to imperil the food supplies.' In that case why did the National Union of Railwaymen, so long ago as Friday last, instruct its members not to handle traffic of any kind, 'food or otherwise'? Why did the workers at the Co-operative Wholesale Sun Flour Mills come out yesterday? Why did several hundred volunteer workers have to unload foodstuffs at the Salford docks? Why did the T.U.C. ask the Dublin dockers, as reported by our Labour correspondent, to place an embargo on foodstuffs to this country? If the T.U.C. wishes people to believe that it is doing nothing to imperil the food supplies it should not confine itself to statements to that effect, but should at once order all of its members engaged upon the manufacture or distribution of foodstuffs to return to work immediately.

p.2

CORRESPONDENCE

AN OUTSIDE MEDIATOR

To the Editor of the Manchester Guardian

Sir,–Sooner or later the trade union leaders may decide to stop the present attempt to bring about a total cessation of work in industries other than coalmines. Indeed, they may be now considering whether lost credit might not be regained for themselves and the Labour party by an announcement that, in order to enable negotiations to be resumed, they withdraw their strike orders. If and when these are withdrawn mediation again becomes possible, and the question arises how this should be conducted. Besides the colliery employers and the miners, a third and fourth body of men have entered the conflict, viz. the Government and the T.U.C. Committee.

After suddenly breaking off the negotiations and then, in face of the general strike, being under the necessity of entering into a struggle with the T.U. leaders, the Prime Minister and his Cabinet colleagues seem to be far less likely to mediate successfully in the coal dispute than some independent person outside all the four bodies mentioned. Therefore it seems that such a person acceptable to each of these four bodies, should be appointed mediator, as indeed was the practice in pre-war disputes.

Mediation by the Premier may have been a necessity in time of war. But its development during the Coalition Government and its maintenance of this form of mediation after the war have appeared to many people to lead to evil consequences. Moreover, mediation in an industrial dispute on a large scale, especially over such a complex problem as that dealt with by the Report of the Coal Commission, should be a whole-time job for a mediator of recognised impartiality. The Premier is necessarily unable to give more than a fraction of his time to a task of this kind. Moreover, if he himself has in the past been regarded as impartial, he has to consult Cabinet colleagues, some of whom, rightly or wrongly, are regarded as anything but impartial.

It seems desirable, therefore, that the view should be pressed on Ministers that mediation should be resumed not by the Government, but by a special whole-time mediator. In a problem of the great complication of the coal dispute the further suggestion might be made that the mediator should be assisted by experts as assessors – probably some, at least, of the same persons who acted in a similar capacity for Sir H. Samuel's Coal Commission.

It might, or might not, be thought advisable to ask Sir H. Samuel himself to act as mediator. If not many names will suggest themselves.–Yours, &c.,

S.
May 9.

THE MINEOWNERS' CHANCE.

To the Editor of the Manchester Guardian.

Sir,–The folly of the Trade Union Council in threatening a general strike, and of the Government in precipitating it by so hastily breaking off negotiations is now apparent in the deadlock with which the country is faced. The Government will not resume negotiations until the strike is called off; the Trade Union Council cannot call off the strike without appearing to desert the miners, to whose support they are pledged; the miners themselves have handed over the conduct of their case to the Trade Union Council, and can do nothing. Alone among the parties to the dispute, the mineowners are in a position, without concession of substance or loss of dignity to invite a resumption of negotiations.

Mr. Baldwin said some very hard things about the mineowners in his House of Commons speech a week ago; if they will now invite the miners to resume negotiations on the basis of the full acceptance of the Commission's report they can turn the tables on Mr. Baldwin by finding a way out of the impasse to which his intervention has led the dispute. By so doing they will demonstrate the ability of the industry to manage its own affairs, make a beginning of the work of restoring that mutual confidence without which prosperity will never be restored, and establish a claim to temporary assistance until prosperity is restored. If the miners accept the invitation – as they must, if they are not to put themselves in the wrong in the eyes of their fellow trade unionists – the Trade Union Council can call off the general strike and the Government will be free to renew its offers of help.

Between the flat refusal of the district delegates of the miners to accept any reduction of wages at all and the owners' proposal of new minimum percentages over standard there are surely possibilities of reducing labour costs which will leave untouched the subsistence wage of the lowest-paid day worker and the guaranteed minimum of the underground piece worker.

Until these have been explored the country is in the dark and the disputants are at cross-purposes. The owners have an opportunity that is open to no one else of removing these uncertainties, and, by a generous gesture, of rehabilitating their reputation with their fellow-countrymen.–Yours, &c.,

OBSERVER.

Manchester, May 9.

p.2

THE PRESSMAN'S BIT.

A paper at last! And its makers
    Can stand to the job that they know,
Can choose between builders and breakers
    And settle which way they will go;
A world that is mostly up-ended,
    For Folly to plunder and rob,
Has a glimpse of the new Vision Splendid –
    The chance to get on with your job.

The tide has seemed long in its turning;
    Not yet is the chance before all,
But the chance for which all men are yearning
    Must lie within very short call;
The chance, not to ruin or fetter,
    But rather to live and let live,

The chance to rebuild and build better,
　　To work and be wise – and forgive.

The paper appears – and we nourish
　　The fact as a sign of release,
A challenge, a fanfare, a flourish,
　　A gesture in favour of peace.
With that as his ultimate message
　　The pressman his readers may greet!
A paper at last – a presage
　　of sanity back in her seat!

LUCIO

p.3

STOP PRESS NEWS

NEW PEACE HOPE.
Premier Meeting T.U.C. Today?

Cabinet sat till 1.15 this morning awaiting message from T.U.C., who had been in conference with miners all night. At 1.15 information reached Premier not to expect T.U.C., but Press Association understands a communication is expected this morning with view to a meeting being arranged to-day. Ministers then dispersed. T.U.C. conference ended 1.35. Miners left 20 minutes before.

Thursday May 13 1926 *p.3*

THE GENERAL STRIKE CALLED OFF.
But Miners' Leaders Reject New Peace Plan.

NO RESERVATIONS IN T.U.C.'S ACTION.
Faith in Scheme Agreed with Sir. H. Samuel.

The T.U.C. General Council called off the general strike yesterday afternoon without reservation 'in order to resume negotiations.' The decision followed the framing of proposals for a coal settlement reached in discussions with Sir Herbert Samuel acting as an independent mediator. The miners' leaders have announced, however, their rejection of the Samuel plan, and their members have been instructed not to return to work pending a delegate conference called for to-morrow.

Mr. Baldwin, who is to meet the mineowners to-day,

announced his intention of proceeding to negotiations without delay, and in a spirit of goodwill and co-operation and without recriminations.

T.U.C. AND MINERS' LEADERS DIVIDED.

(From our Labour Correspondent.)

London, Wednesday.

The general strike has been called off, but the aim for which it was declared is unaccomplished. Sir Herbert Samuel worked out with the General Council of the Trade Unions Congress a basis of negotiation which the miners have rejected. The mining stoppage will go on, but the miners will no longer be able to count on the united support of the trade union movement. The effects on British labour will be profound. The history of 1921 has repeated itself. The support of the other trade unions has been withdrawn. The Government has committed itself to little or nothing. The mineowners are committed to nothing.

It was with full knowledge that the miners would reject the proposals that the General Council decided to call off the general strike. The miners have called the delegate conference for Friday to report on the situation. Its decision will obviously be affected by the Executive's resolution. Feeling to-night among the miners is embittered. The General Council, after nine days of a general strike that has cost all the unions dear, is not less sad that all its efforts have gone for nothing, and that the miners now show even less disposition to compromise than they did a fortnight ago.

Premier and Owners Meet To-day.

The Government is prepared to do its best to get negotiations reopened. Mr. Baldwin has asked the mineowners to see him to-morrow morning. But the miners' rejection of the Samuel proposals makes the outlook unpromising. The mineowners do not like the Samuel proposals, but if the Government, the unions, and the miners had supported them the owners would not have been in a strong position to resist.

Sir Herbert Samuel, the chairman of the Coal Commission, came back from Italy last week-end, and took up the work of mediation. He saw informally the Government, the T.U.C., and the miners. He discussed with the T.U.C. Negotiating Committee yesterday afternoon proposals for a basis of negotiation which would follow the Commission's report in putting reorganisation first and a revision of the wages system second. Last night the General Council and the Miners' Executive discussed these proposals for five and a half hours, and sat until half past one this morning. The

T.U.C. representatives had given the Government to understand that agreement was likely, and Mr. Baldwin, Lord Birkenhead, Mr. Churchill, Lord Balfour, Sir Arthur Steel-Maitland, and other Ministers waited at 10, Downing Street in the expectation that the T.U.C. would wait on them with a proposal for ending the strike. Agreement was not reached last night, although there seemed some hopes of it.

A Last Effort to Persuade the Miners.

This morning the miners met at Russell Square, joined by some members of the General Council, including Mr. Bevin, who made a final attempt to win the miners' acceptance – or, at any rate, to persuade them to hold an open mind on the Samuel proposals. They failed, but the General Council did not alter its decision to call off the strike. Just after noon the full Council went to Downing Street and saw the Prime Minister, Mr. Churchill, Mr. Chamberlain, Mr. Bridgeman, Lord Birkenhead, Sir Arthur Steel-Maitland, Sir Laming Worthington-Evans, and Colonel Lane-Fox. The meeting lasted less than an hour, and when it ended the announcement of the calling off of the strike was made, and the text of the correspondence between Sir Herbert Samuel and the General Council was published.

The verbatim report of the speeches at the interview conveys no impression that either side knew that the miners would not accept the proposals. Mr. Pugh described how the Council recognised that however long the strike lasted negotiations would have to come, and how in reliance on Mr. Baldwin's offer of an open door the Council had explored possibilities, and felt that they could now call off the strike 'in order that negotiations may proceed.' Mr. Baldwin replied, 'I shall lose no time in using every endeavour to get the contending parties together and do all I can to ensure a just and lasting settlement.' Mr. Thomas said that the Council had been moved by a desire to do the right thing.' Mr. Bevin asked the Government to help in the reinstatement of the strikers. The general proposals were not actually discussed and Mr. Baldwin gave no pledge that they would be accepted and supported by the Government.

The Miners' Executive remained sitting at Russell Square. Its first act was to send the telegram to all the districts (printed elsewhere) instructing the miners to await Friday's delegate conference. At five o'clock the Executive issued its reply to the T.U.C. rejecting the Samuel proposals, regretting that 'no opportunity for consideration was afforded the accredited representatives of the Miners' Federation on the negotiating committee in the preparation of the proposals or in the discussion of yesterday which led up to them.' The Executive fastened on the point that wages cuts are 'implied,' and held to its repeated declarations against any reductions.

Late in the afternoon Sir Herbert Samuel explained how his efforts had been directed towards meeting the unions' fear that if their wages were reduced reorganisation would be dropped. Whether the suggested basis would open the way to resumption of negotiations depended on the miners consenting to it. 'If they do not,' summed up Sir Herbert, 'the position as far as the miners are concerned will remain as it was, and the stoppage of the mines will continue. If they do, the Government will, I believe, be fully justified in renewing the subsidy pending negotiations. The mines can then restart, and the discussions that were interrupted be resumed.'

Bewildered Trade Unions.

Midnight.

The trade union movement is in bewilderment to-night. The miners declare that they were rather rushed by the T.U.C. The poor response to the strike call of the shipyard workers (only 25 per cent of whom and on the north-east coast only 5 per cent are said to have come out to-day) and the engineers would provide some reason if it were not that the Council had been preparing for calling off the strike last night. The comparative failure of the Council's policy in relation to food supplies and electrical power may also have counted. There will be recrimination enough on these things later.

Hopes now rest on the miners' delegate conference. If the conference should decide to enter into negotiations the miners' negotiators will find the situation is better in the important respect that the Samuel proposals mark a great step forward. If the conference, as seems likely, refers a decision to the districts or decides to take a ballot on the terms, there is perhaps some hope that the executive's negotiating hands may be untied.

Many interesting questions now arise. What is to be the attitude of the transport unions towards the handling of coal? Is foreign coal to be imported? Will the Continental miners and dockers still maintain their embargo?

T.U.C. MANIFESTO LAST NIGHT.

Coal Settlement Now Possible.

The General Council of the T.U.C. sat all yesterday afternoon, and last night the following statement was issued:–

The General Council through the magnificent support and solidarity of the trade union movement, has obtained assurances that a settlement of the mining problem can be secured which justified them in bringing the general stoppage to an end. . . . The

Government had declared that under no circumstances could negotiations take place until the general strike had been terminated, but the General Council feel as a result of the conversations with Sir Herbert Samuel, and the proposals which are embodied in the correspondence and documents which are enclosed, that sufficient assurances had been obtained as to the lines upon which a settlement could be reached to justify them in terminating the general strike.

The General Council accordingly decided at their meeting to-day to terminate the general stoppage, in order that negotiations could be resumed to secure a settlement in the coal mining industry, free and unfettered from either strike or lock-out. It was felt, having regard to the varied circumstances and practices in each industry, that it would be better for each executive council itself to make arrangements for the resumption of work of its own members.

No attack was at any time contemplated upon the established political institutions of the country. . . . The unions that have maintained so resolutely and unitedly their generous and ungrudging support of the miners can be satisfied that an honourable understanding has been reached. The General Council feel in taking the last steps to bring the crisis to an end that the trade union movement has given a demonstration to the world of discipline, unity and loyalty without parallel in the history of industrial disputes.

p.3

HOW STRIKE WAS CALLED OFF.
T.U.C. Meeting With Premier.

FRANK APPEALS.
Need for Aid in Doing the Big Thing.

The official report was issued last night of the meeting at 10, Downing Street, yesterday, at which the end of the strike was announced. The Trade Unions Congress General Council representatives included Mr. Arthur Pugh (chairman) and Mr. A.B. Swales (vice chairman).

The Prime Minister: Mr. Pugh, will you be good enough to make a statement?

Mr. Pugh: Well, sir, when we separated something over a week ago it was, of course, recognised and expressed on both sides that the ultimate end would be a settlement of this matter by negotiations, and although the conflict has been very much extended and developments have taken place since then, clearly both sides and all sides and all parties have had in view – they must have had – the ultimate arrangements that would have to be made to bring this trouble to a successful end. We, of course, like yourself, have had, despite whatever developments might have taken place – everybody has had, – to direct our thoughts in that channel and to use such opportunities as present themselves and such public opinion as existed with a view to effecting a resumption of negotiations. In that respect, sir, your contribution was made in the statement delivered to the people of the country through the wireless stations. That was something which we, on our side, certainly could not ignore. On the other hand we had been exploring other possibilities with full knowledge that whatever happened, and however long the present position lasted, or whatever might be its consequences in the long run, the process of negotiations would have to be gone through.

Well, as a result of developments in that direction and the possibilities that we see in getting back to negotiations, and your assurance, speaking for the general community of citizens as a whole, that no step should be left unturned to get back to negotiations, we are here to-day, sir, to say that the general strike is to be terminated forthwith in order that negotiations may proceed, and we can only hope may proceed in a manner which will bring about a satisfactory settlement. That is the announcement which my General Council is empowered to make.

The Prime Minister: That is, the general strike is to be called off forthwith?

Mr. Pugh: Forthwith. That means immediately. There is just a point about the actual arrangement, but that is in effect what it means. It is merely a matter of the best way to get it done with the least confusion.

The Premier's Reply.

The Prime Minister: I mean there would be a great deal of work for both of us to do. All I would say in answer to that is I thank God for your decision, and I would only say now I do not think it is a moment for lengthy discussion. I only say now I accept fully and confirm fully all I have said in the last two paragraphs of my broadcasted message. I shall call my Cabinet together forthwith, report to them what you have said, and I shall lose no time using every endeavour to get the two contending parties together and do all I can to ensure a just and lasting settlement. I hope it may be possible before long to make a statement of the lines on which we hope to accomplish that end.

Mr. Thomas: Only one or two of us wish to say anything to you, and it will be very brief. You answered us in the way we knew you would answer us, namely that, just as you recognise we have done a big thing in accepting the responsibility, we felt sure the big thing would be responded to in a big way. We are satisfied all too well that it will not be a day or two, or a week, in which the dislocation and difficulty can be put right; but whatever may be the view of the merits of the dispute now ending there is common agreement that assistance from those who were opposing parties ten minutes ago is essential to rectify and make good and start things on the right road again.

Your assistance in that is necessary, our assistance is necessary. We intend to give it, and in doing that we believe you can help. We want you to help us in that direction. I never liked the word 'war,' and I do not want to use it, but we want your help when this dispute is ended. We trust your word as Prime Minister. We ask you to assist us in the way you only can assist us, by asking employers and all others to make the position as easy and smooth as possible, because the one thing we must not have is guerilla warfare. That must be avoided and in that both sides have to contribute immediately. Nothing could be worse than that this great decision which we have taken should be interpreted otherwise than as a general desire to do the right thing in a difficult moment for the industry of the nation.

The T.U.C.'s Risk.

Mr. Bevan: I think you will agree in the difficulties we have had before us that at least we have taken a great risk in calling the strike off. I want to urge it must not be regarded as an act of weakness, but rather one of strength. I am not talking of strength of muscle and brawn, but rather that it took a little courage to take the lines we have done.

I want to stress Mr. Thomas's point and ask you if you could tell us whether you are prepared to make a general request, as head of the Government, that facilities for reinstatement and that kind of thing shall be given forthwith. The position is this. Some of the undertakings that are affected, of course, are affected by associations which are get-at-able, others are all over the country. When this goes out in the press it may cause untold confusion, but if you could agree with us to make a declaration it would, I think, facilitate matters, and employers, no doubt, have been acting at least in carrying out the spirit of the Government during the fight naturally, and they would no doubt respond to a statement of that character, and I would put it to you very strongly that this is one of the easiest ways of doing things. One of the reasons I want to put it to you is this. In a dislocation of this character it does affect production very much, especially in producing trades, and if there is a resumption with a sort of good feeling, then the thing gets back on to its usual footing very rapidly. If there is not, then it does affect the restoration.

I remember after the 1912 strike when we were beaten Sir Joseph Broodbank went into it very carefully, and the loss in output of transport was something like 25 per cent for some time until the war. We do not want that kind of thing. We have had a row and it does upset things, but we are quite willing to co-operate with our men to repair the damage just as much as the employers, but the employers are the people who can facilitate that kind of feeling, and I am sure they would respond to you if you issued that as a statement.

It would be very helpful to me before we left the building if we could have some indication in that direction, because we shall have to send telegrams to unions whose headquarters are not in London, with whom we cannot converse, and compiling with it a declaration from yourself would in a way give the lead as to how the thing is to be approached. You said, sir, also you were going to call the parties together in order to effect a just settlement.

The Mining Negotiations.

Now we have called our show off and work will be resumed quickly, I do not know whether I am overstepping the bounds, but I would like you to give me an idea of whether that means that there is to be a resumption of the mining operations with us, or whether all the negotiations have to be carried on while the miners still remain out.

Mr. Thomas: That implies that we interpret your speech to mean what I am sure it did mean.

Mr. Bevin: It helped us to rise to the occasion. I thought personally – of course it is so difficult when you have to take it without conversing – I really felt in the event of our taking the lead in assuring you we were going to play the game and put our people back, that it was going to be free and unfettered negotiation with the parties very speedily, because thousands of our people cannot go back if the colliers are still out, and if the colliers are still out it is going to make it extremely difficult to get a smooth running of the machine. Those are the two points I wish to put to you.

Mr. Baldwin's Promises.

The Prime Minister: Well, Mr. Bevin, I cannot say more here at this meeting now. I did not know what points you were going to raise or that anything would be said beyond the statement of Mr. Pugh. The point you have put is one I must consider, and I will consider it at once. I would only say in my view the best thing to do is to get as quickly as possible into touch with the employers. I think that the quicker that is done the less friction there will be. You know my record. You know the object of my policy, and I think you may trust me to consider what has been said with a view to seeing how best we can get the country quickly back into the condition in which we all want to see it.

You will want my co-operation and I shall want yours to try and make good the damage done to the trade and try and make this country a little better and a happier place than it has been in recent years. That will be my steady endeavour, and I look to all of you when we are through this for your co-operation in that. I shall do my part and I have no doubt you will do yours.

In regard to the second point, there again I cannot say at this moment what will happen, because I shall have to see the parties. My object, of course, is to get the mines started the first moment possible and get an agreement reached. I cannot say until I have seen them exactly what the lines will be upon which my object can best be attained, but you may rely on me and rely on the Cabinet, that they will see no step is left untaken to accomplish this end.

Now, Mr. Pugh, as I said before, we have both of us got a great deal to do and a great deal of anxious and difficult work, and I think that the sooner you get to your work and the sooner I get to mine the better.

Mr. Pugh: Yes, that sums up the position for the moment.

Mr. Bevin: I am a little persistent. I do not want to take up your time, but shall we be meeting on these two points soon?

The Prime Minister: I cannot say that, Mr. Bevin. I think it may be that whatever decision I come to the House of Commons may be the best place in which to say it. I cannot say at the moment whether the better thing would be to do it there or meet again, but we are gong to consider right away what is best.

p.3

STRIKE PEACE BASIS.
Text of the Official Announcements.

SIR H. SAMUEL'S MEMORANDUM.
Formula T.U.C. Accepted.

At the conclusion of the conference of the representatives of the Trade Union Congress General Council with the Ministers yesterday the following official statement was given:–

The Prime Minister, who was accompanied by the Minister of Labour, the Secretary for India, the Minister of Health, the Secretary for War, the First Lord of the Admiralty, and the Secretary for Mines, received members of the General Council of the T.U.C. at 12 20 to-day at No. 10, Downing-street. Mr. Pugh announced on behalf of the General Council of the T.U.C. that the general strike was being terminated to-day.

The following announcement on behalf of the General Council of the Trade Unions Congress was broadcast almost immediately afterwards:–

In order to resume negotiations the General Council of the T.U.C. has decided to terminate the general strike to-day, and telegrams of instructions are being sent to the general secretaries of all affiliated unions. Members, before acting, must await the definite instructions from their own executive councils.–(Signed by the Chairman and the Secretary of the T.U.C.)

Sir H. Samuel's Intervention

The T.U.C. General Council also issued shortly afterwards copies of correspondence that had passed between themselves and Sir Herbert Samuel, Chairman of the Royal Commission. In a letter to the General Council, dated May 12, Sir Herbert stated:–

As the outcome of the conversations which I had with your committee I attach a memorandum embodying the conclusions that have been reached. I have made it clear to your committee from the outset that I have been acting entirely on my own initiative, have received no authority from the Government, and can give no assurances on their behalf.

I am of opinion that the proposals embodied in the memorandum are suitable for adoption and are likely to promote a settlement of the differences in the coal industry. I shall strongly recommend their acceptance by the Government when the negotiations are renewed.

To this letter Mr. A. Pugh, the chairman of the General Council, and Mr. W. Citrine, the secretary, replied yesterday, as follows:–

The General Council, having carefully considered your letter of to-day and the memorandum attached to it, concurred in your opinion that it offers a basis on which the negotiations upon the conditions in the coal industry can be renewed. They are taking the necessary measures to terminate the general strike, relying upon the published assurances of the Prime Minister as to the steps that would follow. They assume that during the resumed negotiations the subsidy will be renewed, and that the lock-out notices to the miners will be immediately withdrawn.

The Samuel Memorandum.

The memorandum submitted to the General Council by Sir Herbert Samuel is as follows:–

(1) The negotiations upon the conditions of the coal industry should be resumed, the subsidy being renewed for such reasonable period as may be required for that purpose.

(2) Any negotiations are unlikely to be successful unless they provide for means of settling disputes in the industry other than conferences between the mineowners and the miners alone. A National Wages Board should, therefore, be established which would include representatives of those two parties with a neutral element and an independent chairman. The proposals in this direction tentatively made in the report of the Royal Commission should be pressed and the powers of the proposed Board enlarged.

(3) The parties to the Board should be entitled to raise before it any points they consider relevant to the issue under discussion,

and the Board should be required to take such points into consideration.

(4) There should be no revision of the previous wage rates unless there are sufficient assurances that the measures of re-organisation proposed by the Commission will be effectively adopted. A Committee should be established, as proposed by the Prime Minister – on which representatives of the men should be included, – whose duty it should be to co-operate with the Government in the preparation of the legislative and administrative measures that are required. The same committee, or alternatively the National Wages Board, should assure itself that the necessary steps, so far as they relate to matters within the industry, are not being neglected or unduly postponed.

(5) After these points have been agreed and the Mines National Wages Board has considered every practicable means of meeting such immediate financial difficulties as exist, it may, if that course is found to be absolutely necessary, proceed to the preparation of a wage agreement.

(6) Any such agreement should
    (1) If practicable be on simpler lines than those hitherto followed;
    (2) Not adversely affect in any way the wages of the lowest paid men;
    (3) Fix reasonable figures below which the wage of no class of labour for the normal customary week's work should be reduced in any circumstances;
    (4) In the event of any new adjustment being made should provide for the revision of such adjustments by the Wages Board from time to time if the facts warrant that course.

(7) Measures should be adopted to prevent the recruitment of new workers over the age of eighteen years into the industry if unemployed miners are available.

(8) Workers who are displaced as a consequence of the closing of uneconomic collieries should be provided for by

(a) The transfer of such men as may be mobile, with the Government assistance that may be required, as recommended in the report of the Royal Commission.

(b) The maintenance for such period as may be fixed of those who cannot be so transferred and for whom alternative employment cannot be found, this maintenance to comprise an addition to the existing rate of unemployment pay under the Unemployment Insurance Act of such amount as may be agreed. A contribution should be made by the Treasury to cover the additional sums so disbursed.

(c) The rapid construction of new houses to accommodate the transferred workers. The Trade Unions Congress will facilitate this by consultation and co-operation with all those who are concerned.

126

Miners' Statement.

Shortly after the Miners' Executive had resumed their conference at Russell Square in the afternoon the following official statement was made:–

The Miners' Executive met this morning and discussed the position after a deputation from the Trade Unions Council had visited them, when they decided to reaffirm their previous position. The following telegram has been sent to all the districts: 'Miners must not resume work pending decision of National Delegate Conference convened for Friday next at Kingsway Hall, London, 10 a.m. Plese send delegates.–(Signed) Cook, Secretary.'

It is my intention and my colleagues' intention (Mr. Cook proceeded) to report fully to the National Conference. It will be for the men to decide what action they will take after the report has been given and in the light of the circumstances. As far as we are concerned, we still stand for maintaining our present position.

p.3

HOW SETTLEMENT WAS ANNOUNCED.
Downing Street Scenes.

WILD WELCOME TO THE PREMIER.

(From our London Staff.)

Fleet Street, Wednesday.

The first announcement of the settlement was made to a large and cosmopolitan gathering of journalists in 10, Downing Street. While they were waiting Mr. J.H. Thomas came out with the look of a man both bewildered and depressed. He walked in complete silence through the journalists and departed, no one venturing to ask him a question. Soon afterwards all the T.U.C. leaders came out in a body. They too all seemed very depressed, and obviously in no mood for saying anything.

About ten minutes past one a Government official came out with a piece of paper in his hand, and with him was Mr. Citrine, secretary of the Trade Unions Congress. This was the news. The journalists flocked round with the greatest eagerness. The agreed statement which he read was simply a list of the Ministers who had been present, followed by this sentence:

Mr. Pugh announced on behalf of the General Council of the Trade Unions Congress that the general strike is being terminated to-day.

127

'Is it unconditional?' asked an excited foreign journalist. The official did not reply. Half the journalists made a dive to the door, thinking that there was nothing more, but Mr. Citrine had the T.U.C. announcement to read, beginning: 'In order to resume negotiations,' etc. While this was going on Mr. Churchill with a cheerful smile disappeared into his own house.

In the afternoon there was a big crowd in Whitehall to see Mr. Baldwin leave for the House of Commons. When he came out of his house he found himself confronted by about a hundred camera men and kinematographers. 'I say,' he exclaimed, and hesitated in surprise. He was about to get into his car when Mrs. Winston Churchill came running out of No. 11, waving her hand and shouting 'Hooray!' Mr. Baldwin shook hands with her, and the people in the street raised a very hearty cheer for him, and there were shouts of 'Good old Baldwin.' When the car reached the bottom of Downing Street quite a big crowd surged round it, and it had to stop for a moment until the police could clear a way. Then people ran after the car shouting and waving all the way down to the House.

In normal times the news would have been shouted by the newspaper sellers all over London within a few minutes. As it was it penetrated slowly. The first general dissemination of the news was made by wireless and probably reached listeners-in before it was known generally in the middle of London.

p.3

THE PEACE NEWS IN MANCHESTER.
Tramwaymen Intended to Remain Out.

MARCH THROUGH CITY.

Manchester received the news that the general strike had been called off, somewhat incredulously, about the time that it finished its lunch. First word came from those who had access to the one o'clock wireless announcement, and confirmation quickly followed in a special edition of the evening paper bulletins.

In the latest overnight news, and particularly in the stop-press of the 'Manchester Guardian,' some hope had been indicated that negotiation was at last on foot again, but so far as the strike itself was concerned there was little evidence in Manchester of the 'turn of the tide' of which so much had been made by the Government publications. It was realised in the morning that in South-east Lancashire, at any rate, full effect was being given to the decision to extend the strike to the engineers, and there were early reports of the big engineering works in Manchester being stopped, though the engineers at the gasworks had agreed to carry on.

The Manchester tramwaymen had also shown in the morning that they were still solidly behind the strike. At the hour at which they had been required to report for duty (before the peace news was received), a bare handful of them – fifteen men and fourteen boys out of some 5,000 – turned up at the depots. The others came to Hyde Road in full strength, but not to report for duty; from Hyde Road they marched in a procession of several thousands into the centre of the city, headed by their band, and carrying banners which declared their determination to support the cause of the miners. A great many of the tramwaymen were wearing war medals, and on their march into town they were joined by various contingents of other men on strike, until the procession, marching four abreast, was little short of half a mile long.

MANCHESTER TRAMS: FULL SERVICE TO-DAY.

It is hoped that Manchester will have a normal service of trams to-day. The news of the settlement was officially communicated to the local leaders of the tramwaymen by the T.U.C. yesterday afternoon. It was not found possible to run the all-night cars which normally serve Manchester from midnight onwards, but with this exception the men were instructed by their local officials to report for duty at their usual times to-day. The first of the workmen's cars were therefore expected to leave the sheds between four and five this morning.

NO SALFORD CABS TO-DAY.

The Salford tramwaymen decided not to turn in to work this morning, difficulty having arisen because the management were not prepared with a full complement of cars and could not take all the men back at once.

PARCEL POST RESTORED.

The Manchester Post Office announces that the inland and foreign parcel post has been re-established and that the restriction as regards the weight of packets has been removed.

MANCHESTER TRAIN SERVICES.

The normal working of trains from Manchester terminal cannot be resumed on either the L.M.S. or L.N.E.R. systems to-day. The temporary services, particulars of which were given in yesterday's 'Manchester Guardian,' will therefore remain in operation to-day.

GLASGOW'S RELIEF.
The Unwilling 'Second Line.'

(From our Special Correspondent.)

Glasgow, Wednesday.

The news that the general strike had been called off created a profound sense of relief in Glasgow. Work at all the shipyards had ceased this morning, and at all the engineering shops with the exception of one large establishment on the lower reaches of the Clyde. The men in these industries had struck very unwillingly, and they were glad to learn that no serious strain was to be imposed upon their trade union loyalty.

It is expected that they will all resume work to-morrow. At the same time a good deal of uneasiness was expressed in trade union circles concerning the fate of the miners.

Glasgow has come through the period of the general strike very well. It is true there has been a good deal of disorder. About 300 persons altogether have been arrested for riotous conduct and breaches of the peace, but everyone who knows the city well agrees that 75 per cent of the people arrested were not directly concerned in the strike but belonged to the hooligan class with whom the police are waging continual warfare.

The police have done admirably. They appear to have cowed the lawless elements of the population completely, for there has been no disorder in the city since Saturday night. Perhaps the worst incident reported since the strike began was an act of sabotage on the railway between Glasgow and Dumfries. Strikers tore up a part of the track and to-day there has been no communication between St. Enoch's Station, Glasgow, and Dumfries.

p.2

Leader   # THE END OF THE GENERAL STRIKE

With great thankfulness and no little pride in the steadiness with which it has endured a terrible ordeal the country will to-day take up the threads of its ordinary life. For this result we are chiefly indebted to the chairman of the Coal Commission, Sir Herbert Samuel, to whose efforts as unofficial mediator the country owes as deep a debt of gratitude as it does for his work on the Commission itself. The strike orders have been withdrawn unconditionally. In withdrawing them the Trade Unions Council has relied upon Sir Herbert Samuel's assurance that he will do his utmost to induce the Government to resume negotiations on the basis which he outlines and which the T.U.C. endorses. No more satisfactory solution could well have been found. The general strike has been ended without any recognition by the Government of the authority of the strikers to bargain with the State. The essential basis of representative government has been fully and formally maintained. On the other hand, the Trade Unions Council has not pushed matters to the last extremes of exhaustion of either its own or the country's resources. It might have done so had it not had confidence in Sir Herbert Samuel's capacity to induce the Government to accept his suggestions for the renewal of negotiations. But that confidence was based upon knowledge of Sir Herbert Samuel's character and authority and upon trust, which events are not likely to disabuse, in Mr. Baldwin's determination, once the threat of a general strike is removed, to negotiate in a spirit of sympathy and goodwill. It was not based upon any previous conditions extracted from the Government.

Unhappily, the ending of the general strike does not necessarily imply the ending of the lock-out in the coalfields. At the moment, indeed, the prospect of a resumption of work in the mining industry is far from bright. The miners will not make their formal decision until the National Delegate Conference meets to-morrow, but in the meantime the Executive of the Federation have rejected the Samuel proposals. They still stand rigidly, perhaps even more rigidly than a fortnight ago, by the old standards of wages. If the miners are determined that no reductions whatever shall be made in wages it is difficult to see how a protracted stoppage in the industry is to be avoided. A stoppage must be essentially futile, because the majority of existing mines cannot pay the old rates and it is politically impossible, even if it were desirable, that the Government should continue to pay wages out of the taxes. If the miners persist in this attitude they will fight not only without the active support of other trade unionists but without much of the sympathy which they have hitherto received. The hard case of the miners is genuine enough, though it is no harder than that of the workers in some other industries. But facts have to be faced, and no one, least of all the miners themselves, has yet been able to suggest any fairer or less painful way of meeting them than that of the Coal Commission. It is true that the Commission's Report was distorted in the terms offered by the owners, but that defect is remedied in the Samuel proposals, which, naturally enough, interpret the Report with as strict regard for those parts of it which benefit the miners as for those by which they must lose. If the miners' leaders cannot accept that, and cannot suggest any practicable alternative, they are wilfully blind.

We need not, perhaps, despair of an early settlement even of the mining dispute. That is a matter to which the Government can now give its undivided attention. For the moment it is sufficient to know that the general strike is a thing of the past. What has it accomplished? In a material sense obviously nothing, and far worse than nothing. But has it not taught a lesson which, properly taken to heart, may be worth even its incalculable material losses? Is there any sane man in this country who to-day believes that a general strike of workers in the key industries can be of possible benefit to them or to others? Will not the general strike cease to be counted henceforth as a possible or legitimate weapon of industrial warfare? May not the very idea of treating industry as a theatre of war come to be regarded as barbaric? It is possible, at all events, to hope that this generation will not see a repetition of the supreme follies of last week. But the lesson is not wholly one-sided. It has its warnings for the employers as much as for the employed. They, as well as the workmen, have to build afresh on better and surer foundations. The work of reconstruction will be laborious. It will need the co-operation of all and the fixed resolve to forget the feuds of the past. The King and the Prime Minister have issued appeals for the spirit of generosity which alone can make this possible. If the employers respond to these appeals it may be that industrial relationships in the future will be happier as well as more profitable than in the past. They have a unique opportunity and immense power. Used vindictively it will be wasted. Used not with merely careless benevolence but with careful thought for the best means of developing the essential sense of partnership in industry it may prove to be a boon and a turning point in our industrial history.

p.2

KING'S MESSAGE.
'Let us Forget and Face our Task.'

The following message from the King was issued last night:–

Buckingham Palace.

To my people.

The nation has just passed through a period of extreme anxiety. It was to-day announced that the general strike had been brought to an end. At such a moment it is supremely important to bring together all my people to confront the difficult situation which still remains.

This task requires the co-operation of all able and well disposed men in the country. Even with such help it will be difficult, but it will not be impossible. Let us forget whatever elements of bitterness the events of the past few days may have created, only remembering how steady and how orderly the country has remained though severely tested, and forthwith address ourselves to the task of bringing into being a peace which will be lasting because, forgetting the past, it looks only to the future with the hopefulness of a united people.

(Signed) George R.I.

TAKING BACK STRIKERS
Government Statement.

The following official statement was issued last night:–

His Majesty's Government have no power to compel employers to take back every man who has been on strike, nor have they entered into any obligation of any kind in this matter. Some displacements are inevitable in view of the reduction of business consequent upon the strike as well as any obligations which may have been entered into by employers towards volunteers who have helped them during the last week.

Attention is, however, drawn to the hope expressed by the Prime Minister in his statement in the House of Commons 'that we should resume our work in a spirit of co-operation, putting behind us all malice and all vindictiveness.' The best course is for the various trade unions to get into immediate touch with the association of employers concerned in order that if possible a satisfactory agreement may be reached.

RIOT AT DONCASTER
80 Men Arrested After Police Charge.

Doncaster coalfield was the scene of serious disorder yesterday afternoon as the result of which over eighty miners were arrested. Two hundred miners held up the traffic, wrecking a newspaper van, destroying newspapers, and looting motor-lorries. The police charged the crowd with truncheons. They were reinforced by mounted men, who scattered the rioters. The arrested men were conveyed to Doncaster in motor-'buses.

OUR LONDON CORRESPONDENCE

(By Private Wire.)

London, Wednesday night.

THE UNCOMMITTED GOVERNMENT.

In all Government communiques and communications it is insisted upon, with every variety of phraseology, that the withdrawal of the strike orders was unconditional, that there was no undertaking, explicit or implied, to renew the subsidy or to renew negotiations or anything else except what had already been announced in the statements made before – and, one may add, since – the breakdown.

It is true, and it is a good thing that it should be true, and no one need examine too closely into the precise antecedents of a supremely fortunate result. It is sufficient that the Labour people are willing to stake everything on Sir Herbert Samuel's prescience, and we must all hope that their confidence may be justified.

CONDITIONS OF THE UNCONDITIONAL SURRENDER.

It only remains to say with much satisfaction that the spokesmen of the Government formally and informally agree that the Government stands by all its promises as to the resumption of negotiations. It is not going back on anything, and the last thing it would go back upon is the Coal Report as the basis of settlement. There is every reason to expect that the negotiations really will be resumed, if not where they were broken off on Friday night, April 30, or on Sunday night, May 2, then a stage farther on, for Sir Herbert Samuel's memorandum, accepted by the Trade Unions Congress, is a stage farther on.

It is generally believed among Labour members that behind to-day's dealings between the T.U.C. and the Government there lies what one Labour member described to me as a 'gentleman's agreement.' One need not press this too far. The Government are going to renew negotiations, and if there is any reasonable prospect of its doing good they will certainly renew the subsidy in some form for a short time.

To-day's Cabinet meeting was at 2 30, and only lasted a quarter of an hour. It was merely to make the formal announcement to the whole Cabinet of what had happened. The real Cabinet meeting on the subject will be held at 11 o'clock to-morrow morning. In the same way Mr. Baldwin said only a few conciliatory and generous sentences in the House of Commons to-day. The real statement and debate will be later this week, probably to-morrow.

DEMOBILISATION.

The Government will put an end to the state of emergency and to the regulations under the proclamation as speedily as possible, but it is clear that it must take a little time. Demobilisation of the volunteer workers and special constables will be begun as soon as possible. Recruiting for these two services will stop at once, but there will be no disbanding for the moment. For one thing the Government will wait for the necessary time to be sure, as it is expressed, that the goods will be delivered, for it is easier to call men out on strike than to get them all back to work.

The emergency orders of the Mines Department will remain in force as long as the coal dispute lasts – that is, all the orders arising out of the stoppage of the production of coal. There are also a good many contracts and odds and ends of the mobilisation of the last week that will have to be wound up. The proclamation of emergency, it may be recalled, was signed on the night of Friday, April 30, before the general strike was actually ordered.

I am authoritatively informed that the Government will take the initiative in resuming negotiations. As soon as they are convinced that the general strike is definitely finished and that the normal condition of affairs is being gradually resumed they will move to get the two sides together again.

HOW THE WAR WON THE STRIKE.

Undoubtedly the war increased the community's power of resistance. The difference was that the new habit of mind and executive capacity of the middle classes, and the comradeship which still persists in the minds of both strikers and volunteers, was a big factor in the unparalleled pacific character of this great conflict, which has really been the wonder of the world. Both points worked against the strikers. Another point was the new middle-class women, fitted by experience and training to conditions and labour that in most cases would have shocked and incapacitated her mother. This all went in one direction, for those who sympathised with the strike could do little to help to stop things, while in helping cheerfully to overcome the difficulties and be helpful women were following their natural desires.

A generation ago it was all rather different. The average middle-class Englishman of twenty years ago, after generations of peace with vast resources of menial labour, could do little except sport with his hands and had not the habit of mind for discipline and adaptability. The Boer War proved it, the Great War cured it. Men learnt that instead of writing letters to the press when things were not done that they could go and do them themselves. The way to get a thing done was to do it.

WAR COMRADES IN CONFLICT.

Many false class conceptions died, too. It is only men too old to have been in the war who now talk of 'teaching the workmen the lesson they deserve' and 'making them lick it,' and all the ugly, futile old slogans of the stonehenges of the past. The volunteers went on driving 'buses, loading food, and the rest of it, and the strikers went on trying to prevent them, but there was with most of them a sort of understanding that never existed before, and they had a common trench language they never had before. How long this thread between them would have lasted in the sharper conflict of another week one cannot surmise, but, happily, the real test never came.

On both sides this was a conflict between men who knew all about arms and bloodshed, and it has ended without bloodshed. Before the war they would have known little about bloodshed, and less about one another. In the struggle the fools on both sides have been miraculously held in check. Are both sides of these sometime comrades to lose also the industrial peace?

On Friday May 14 the Manchester Guardian was still restricted to a four-page issue. In general the industrial situation was still confused despite the ending of the strike. In the regions most of the major unions confronted with threats of victimisation of strike leaders and redefinition of terms of service elected to continue to strike until a satisfactory truce could be negotiated.

Friday May 14 1926   *p.3*

CONFUSION AFTER THE STRIKE.
No General Return to Work.

UNIONS ORDER RAILWAYMEN TO REMAIN OUT.
Reinstatement Troubles.

FIRST STEP TO NEW COAL NEGOTIATIONS

Though the general strike was called off on Wednesday, the position last night was that most of the unions affected remained out on what may be called sectional strikes.

Tramwaymen returned in many towns. But the railway companies laid down certain conditions, for reinstatement, and the unions ordered their members to remain on strike. Last night there was a conference between the union leaders and the railway managers, but no agreement was reached and the discussions will be continued this morning.

The dockers also remain out in London, Manchester, Liverpool, and Hull, and the newspaper industry was another in which there was no general resumption.

The conditions of reinstatement offered by the employers in almost every case made no change in hours or wages. The T.U.C. issued a manifesto last night declaring that some employers were 'seizing the opportunity to attack trade unionism' and promising determined resistance. In the House of Commons Mr. Baldwin in a vigorous speech declared that he would not countenance any attempts on the part of employers to use the occasion for trying to get reductions of wages or increase in hours.

Late last night the first step to renewed coal negotiations was taken when the Premier met the Miners' Executive.

THE COLLAPSE AND ITS SEQUEL.

(From our Labour Correspondent.)

London, Thursday.

The General Council of the Trade Unions Congress, having broken with the miners and called off the general strike, is now entangled in serious difficulties over the reinstatement of the strikers. Important sections of employers are propounding new terms of re-engagement.

The railway companies have informed their workers that reduced staffs only will be taken on, and that those who are taken back will only be employed with reservations. The railway unions have ordered their men to continue on strike 'until we receive satisfactory assurances.' The port employers have taken up the same position as the railway companies, and are 'unable to guarantee' full reinstatement. The dockers and other large sections of workers in other industries remain out.

There seem to be few cases of interference with hours or wages – although Mr. Thomas quoted some in the House to-night. Employers are asking for individual contracts imposing conditions on their workpeople, are turning away any redundant workers, and are discriminating against strikers who have been guilty of intimidation. The position should be eased by Mr. Baldwin's speech to-night with its strong declaration against alterations of hours and wages and its appeal for an early restoration of normal working. He admitted the difficulty of meeting his pledge that volunteers and non-strikers should not suffer. He refused to countenance any attack on the unions and appealed to employers to meet the unions in a friendly spirit to settle reinstatement conditions. Until these meetings have been held the strike will go on on a big scale, but it will be under the control of the executives of individual unions and not of the General Council. It has ceased to be a general strike and has become an aggregation of sectional strikes.

The General Council has told the unions that 'it is imperative that agreements, understandings, and conditions existing before the dispute should be maintained,' and asks them to get in touch with employers and employers' unions and arrange for resumption of work in the spirit of the Prime Minister's broadcast message. Members are urged to sign no individual agreements, but to rely on their union, 'which will protect you and will insist that all agreements previously in force shall be maintained intact.' In a bellicose statement to the public the General Council complains that employers 'are breaking an obligation of honour,' and reiterates that the movement is not broken, 'its strength is unimpaired,' it is 'not suing for mercy,' but if employers continue the unions will 'resist to the utmost.'

The General Council's language reads strangely in the light of its recent actions, which broke all agreements and understandings. It will be noted that none of its statements makes any reference to the miners. The miners have been left to make their own peace. The General Council threw in its hand yesterday and capitulated with a haste and a completeness which did not even gain them the specific assurance of the Government that return on the old terms should follow the surrender.

It is argued to-day that the trade unions really did quite well in bringing out the Samuel proposals. The correspondence between the Government and Sir Herbert Samuel issued to-day makes it more clear than ever that the Government in no way bound itself, and that the mineowners are still to be approached. The General Council had no assurance that the Samuel proposals would be accepted by any of the three parties when the strike was called off.

While the General Council is trying to extricate itself from the pit it has dug the government is moving to revive peace negotiations in the coal industry. The Cabinet considered the situation this morning, and Mr. Baldwin asked the owners and miners to see him to-day.

He was not able to see the owners during the day as he had arranged, but the Miners' Executive met him at half-past nine to-night.

An official statement after the meeting stated that after a general discussion it was adjourned. It is understood Mr. Baldwin will meet the owners to-day.

The Miners' Executive is unable to join in any negotiations until the delegate conference has reviewed the situation. The conference is called for to-morrow, but owing to the difficulty of getting all the delegates in from the country at such short notice it may be postponed until Monday. The course of action which the conference seems likely to take is to empower the executive to take part in reopened negotiations with the owners and the Government on the basis of the maintenance of present wages for a period until reorganisation proposals and a new wages agreement are worked out.

The executive is not as unreasonable on the question of the length of this period as has been suggested, and two or three months would probably be long enough for the advisory committee or National Wages Board to work out a scheme. In the negotiations not only the Samuel proposals but others of related scope and character would be considered.

The Split with the Miners.

The miners are ready to admit that the Samuel proposals are an advance, and contain a great deal that is valuable and adopt the right method of approach to the wages question. The reasons why the executive yesterday rejected them are to be found, I think, largely in the way in which they were presented by the General Council. Here lies the cause of the split with the General Council and the collapse of the general strike.

The full story of this amazing episode will be a subject for many historians. There is very much that is still obscure. The General Council, although it declared the general strike, feared the monster it had created. The strength of the strike resided not in Eccleston Square, with its not very efficient organisation, but in the country in the solidarity of the rank and file. The leaders lost no chance of trying to end the strike. They made bid after bid in Parliament. They saw many would-be mediators. When Sir Herbert Samuel returned, the General Council leaders met him on successive days.

On Monday evening proposals were put to the miners, but refused by them because the Council insisted among other things that the miners must agree to accept a reduction in wages. On Tuesday the long meetings between the Council and Sir Herbert Samuel took place at which the proposals were finally framed. It was not until after eight o'clock that night that the miners saw the full draft. It was put before them, they complain, as an ultimatum. They wished to know whether the terms could be altered, whether they could be discussed by a sub-committee. They were told, it is said, that they were unalterable, that the Council had decided to approach the Prime Minister with them as a basis of settlement.

The Miners' Executive then met separately and passed the resolution rejecting the proposals. At that time, the miners say, they did not know that the General Council had decided to call off the general strike. The Cabinet had, however, been informed that some such event was likely, and waited up until half-past one in the morning.

Yesterday morning a deputation from the General Council met the miners again, but both sides took up the same positions as the night before. This was the first intimation to the miners that the strike was to be called off at midday. While the Council deputation was there the Miners' Executive passed the second resolution re-affirming that of the night before, expressing its admiration of the strikers 'who withdrew' their labour in support of the miners' standards,' and undertaking to report to a delegate conference. The General Council went straight to Downing Street, and in calling off the strike trusted to the generosity of Mr. Baldwin to save them from all consequences.

This is obviously a partial summary, but until the General Council explains its motives more clearly one cannot add much to it in elucidation of the Council's part in the episode.

p.3

AS THE WORLD SEES US.

ITALY.

European Anxiety on Coal Settlements.

(From our own Correspondent.)

Rome, Tuesday.

The Fascist press sees the end of the strike as a resounding victory for law and order over subversive tendencies. Mr. Baldwin is depicted as having rightly held out against the pacifist and 'defeatist' proposals of the Archbishop of Canterbury, Mr. Lloyd George and Sir John Simon, and has been rewarded by a clear and unconditional victory. The 'Messaggero' points out that the coal crisis remains open in all its gravity, and declares that all Europe will await with anxiety the British Government's steps for resolving it, especially since, if the remedy is sought in protective duties, as is probable, the remainder of Europe will have to take a share in the burden. The great lesson of the strike for the 'Messaggero' has been that the British governing classes, represented by Mr. Baldwin's Government, have not yet lost resilience and capacity.

FRENCH PERPLEXITIES.

Commentators Nonplussed by British Calm.

(From our own Correspondent.)

Paris, Wednesday.

Rarely have the French people, usually so insular, been so passionately excited over a crisis in another country as they have been over the British general strike. No words of praise can be too warm for the manner, the objectivity and even kindliness with which French reporters in London have done their work during the last eight days. But from beginning to end the leader-writers in Paris have been sadly perplexed. To think of all these paradoxes – the pound soaring to unprecedented heights when under similar circumstances in France there would have been a panic and a catastrophic drop in the franc exchange; the firmness of all stocks on the London Stock Exchange, while it was the Paris Bourse that was perturbed; strangest of all, the Church apparently taking the part of the working class; or, again, the complete calm, for example, last Sunday in London, while there was bloody rioting in the heart of Paris.

In France, as anywhere else in Europe, such a widespread stoppage would have meant a revolution. How was it possible, despite all the plain facts to the contrary, that it would not possess that character in England? In short, every conceivable instinct and prejudice of the ordinary French politician has been violated by this extraordinary and inexplicable event across the Channel. And the end seems as paradoxical and puzzling as the beginning, so that the commentators can make nothing of it nor be sure which side has won, nor attempt to prophesy the social and political consequences. Consequently the general conclusion is that the British are a people apart, not subject to ordinary rules.

p.3

CONFUSION AT LIVERPOOL.
Volunteers Withdraw, but Strikers Still Out.

Liverpool yesterday shared in the confusion that has occurred all over the country following the calling off of the general strike. Fearing that some of their fellows would be victimised, men in all directions refused to resume work, pending a guarantee that all would be taken back. Thus, the volunteer workers having been withdrawn, there was less work being done than on any day since the strike began.

141

When it was announced that the state of emergency continued the following notice was displayed at Liverpool Town Hall:—

'All traders engaged in emergency services, such as food, docks, shipping, flour milling, railways, &c., are informed that abundant labour can be obtained at the Town Hall on application.'

It was stated later that notices have been posted informing dockers that they may return to work at the old rates.

p.3

GENERAL WORKERS' UNION'S INSTRUCTIONS.

The 'British Worker' announces that the National Union of General and Municipal Workers has instructed its branches that there shall not be any general resumption of work by its members until trade union agreements have been fully recognised.

The Workers' Union has sent messages to its branches as follows: 'Where employers meet in a spirit of reconciliation the men to return to work at once, but members are not to resume work in any firm where there is any attempt on the part of the employers to insist on new agreements or to victimise members.'

p.3

THE GOVERNMENT AND SIR H. SAMUEL.
His Role Entirely Unofficial.

The Labour Ministry yesterday issued the correspondence between Sir Herbert Samuel and the Minister in order to remove misapprehensions to the effect that the Samuel memorandum was in any way authorised by or previously known to the Government. Sir A. Steel-Maitland, writing on May 8, says:—

'Until the necessary orders have been given to withdraw the strike or unless the strike has come to an end, we cannot as a condition or inducement take part in negotiations in relation to the mining issue. For if we did so there would and could be no unconditional withdrawal of the strike notices. On the contrary, the true situation sincerely faced would be that we had procured the end of the general strike by a process of bargaining.

'The Government cannot enter upon any negotiations unless the strike is so unreservedly concluded that there is not even an implication of such a bargain upon their side as would embarrass them in any legislation which they may conceive to be proper in the light of recent events. . . . In these circumstances I am sure that

142

the Government will take the view that while they are bound most carefully and most sympathetically to consider the terms of any arrangement which a public man of your responsibility and experience may propose, it is imperative to make it plain that any discussion which you think proper to initiate is not clothed in even a vestige of official character.'

For futher details of Steel-Maitland see the 'Guide to the Major Characters'.

p.2

Leader # THE WRECKAGE.

It is not going to be an easy matter to clear up the debris of war. The general strike is over, let us hope never to be repeated, but the return to work is sporadic and hampered by all kinds of difficulties which cannot be overcome by a stroke of the pen. The most serious trouble is on the railways, but similar troubles are being experienced in many other industries. Men cannot leave work and demand as a right that they shall all be taken on at a moment's notice as if nothing had happened. Industry has been severely shaken, and some trades will take time to recover. Allowance must be made for the diminished quantity of work that there may be to do. Apart from that, both the unions and employers want to preserve some kind of uniformity in whatever terms are reached, and reference to headquarters takes time. On both sides there is need for much forbearance. We doubt the wisdom, for instance, of the reservation by the railway companies of the right to take action against men who have been guilty of acts of violence and intimidation. Such acts ought to have been dealt with in the courts already. If they have not it is needlessly severe to bring them up now. It is reasonable that the railways should only take on such men as they can find work for, but the conditions which they are seeking to impose appear to be harsh and to leave the door open to the victimisation which the King and Mr. Baldwin have alike deprecated. There can be no peace along that road. The fair terms of reinstatement differ as between different trades and different firms, and it is impossible to generalise. All that can be said is, in the words of the Prime Minister, that we must 'put behind us all malice and all vindictiveness.' It is the future, not the past, which matters, and if employers take what risks they can afford in the reinstatement of their staffs the workers cannot complain if, in consequence of their own actions, these staffs must in some cases or temporarily be a little smaller than they were.

The manifesto issued by the Trade Unions Council shows clearly what is likely to be the effect of any attempt to take undue advantage of the collapse of the general strike. The strike failed, in the main, because the vast majority of the general public condemned it and a large proportion of the strikers themselves had no heart in it. They were willing to follow their unions, but saw little prospect of helping the miners and had, of course, no idea of helping themselves. It was a strike of loyalty, not of conviction. Moreover, the Trade Unions Council did not carry the fight to a finish. They may have known that they would be beaten, but they were not actually beaten when they withdrew the strike notices. All these things will be changed if the conflict is allowed to persist. The railwaymen, for instance, who remain out are not now fighting for a vague ideal of comradeship, but for some definite personal rights of their own. The public which utterly condemned their action in striking in the first instance will have no sympathy for any action by the companies which needlessly keeps them out when they are willing to return. And the Trade Unions Council, which acted with courage and moderation in the final event by calling the strike off before being absolutely compelled, will, as the text of this memorandum shows, display a different temper if the employers themselves become the aggressors. For the injury to trade which they have caused the unions must suffer, and no responsible trade union leader can complain of that fact. But beyond making whatever readjustments are necessary to meet the altered circumstances of trade the employers need not go.

The Trade Unions Council appeal to the Prime Minister to prevent employers from trying 'to victimise and humiliate' the workers who now wish to come back. The Prime Minister has already done much by his appeal on Thursday night 'to forget all recrimination.' The King, Mr. Baldwin, and the Archbishop of Canterbury have all done their best to set negotiations on the right lines, and it now rests with those individually concerned on both sides to carry their words into effect. It is not a matter on which Parliament or the Government can effectively intervene. The first thing to be done is to get work going. No doubt the temptation will be strong in some cases to take advantage of the opportunity to revise agreements as to either wages or working conditions. But revision of agreements takes a long time, and agreements which are improvised or dictated are not usually worth the paper they are written on. It may well be that one of the most important consequences of the strike will be to turn men's minds to different methods of settling industrial disputes. It is even possible that new methods may require Parliamentary assistance. But it seems safe to say that it would be wrong to make revision a condition of restarting work and until business has again been restored to normal. Still less would it be right to attempt to snatch any fleeting advantage which the present collapse of the general strike may seem to offer. The first day of what should have been peace has brought out its difficulties. But it only requires a brief extension of the admirable spirit of reasonableness which prevailed during the strike to set things going again.

p.2

OUR LONDON CORRESPONDENCE

(By Private Wire.)

London, Thursday Night.

THE AFTERMATH.

This has been a shattering day after the great relief of yesterday's calling off of the strike. Even in the middle of the war there were never so many contradictory reports and alarmist statements, nearly all false.

First we heard that the railway companies and the L.C.C. tramways and the London General Omnibus Company were refusing to take the men back in their former status, but only as beginners. It was not till Mr. Baldwin's statement to-night that the story was even questioned. It got general credence and at once affected many volunteers, who made it clear that they would not continue their work if it was not the straightforward settlement that everyone expected. 'We will not take part in a pursuit' was how one of the ex-soldier volunteers put it. The feeling that there were some employers who wanted to turn the general strike surrender into a rout, with lancer work on the disorganised contingents, went completely against the grain of the volunteers who had come out for the national need and not for the cause of any employers.

There were troubles in the tramways to-day. The trams were stoned at Hampstead, and there has been a revivial of disturbances at one or two points. Many volunteers did not turn up to-day in the belief that the workmen would be back, with the result that transport has been much worse in London than for the last four days. There are, however, abundance of taxicabs for those who can pay for them.

On the whole it has been an anxious and unpleasant a day as any in the strike.

LABOUR COUNCILS AND ELECTRICITY.

A good deal of extra unemployment has been caused in the East End by the action of the Stepney Council in restricting the supply of electricity. The workers in the Stepney municipal power house were not actually called out, but power was not supplied except between eight at night and five in the morning. The result of this was to stop many factories and also to cause difficulties at hospitals and public institutions and a part of the docks.

The Council – it has, of course, a Labour majority – is under statutory necessity to supply light and power, and it was threatened with legal action by many consumers for breach of contract. Last night the Transport Ministry sent a circular to the Council reminding it of its legal obligation to supply power at all times and pointing out the penalties that might be enforced for failing to do so. The normal supply of power has now been resumed.

I am told that the same policy of limitation was adopted in other parts of London where there is a Labour council.

SIGHTS OF THE STRIKE.

A few of the strange sights of the strike may be set down. An old stage coach with two horses was hired by a city firm to take their clerks to the office. Several men went to business on horseback. A tall man was seen in Holborn on a child's 'scooter.' No bookmakers were visible in the by-streets.

Volunteer conductors said good-bye to passengers when they got off, and passengers said things like 'Well, we've had a fine time together, haven't we, going from Fleet Street to Charing Cross! Well, good-bye.' Some 'buses to-day carried a broom on deck like Van Tromp. On some days all the newspapers selling in Fleet Street came from Sheffield, Leeds, and Cardiff. A motorist going fifty miles an hour on the Bedford Road was waved on by a policeman to hurry up a bit (a potato convoy was coming up a side road).

A 'bus with volunteer driver pulled up at his house in Eaton Square, and the driver and conductor, who had been out all night, went in for breakfast, then remembered that they had a passenger, and the passenger was induced to join them at breakfast.

An American girl who arrived at Glasgow had a strange trip to London. She got a train to Carlisle, then with a dozen others set out in a motor-coach for Preston, whence a London train was to run. The driver lost the way, and reached Appleby in rain with night coming on. A council was held, and they decided to carry on for London. The driver hit the Great North Road, but lost it before Peterborough, reached Gainsborough, knocking up sleepy people in small towns for directions, and floundered south in the night making leeway to the west at last bringing up in the Thames Valley and so to London.

The temporary London newsellers had their wits about them. An hour after the strike was called off they were crying, 'The dyly piper, one penny; souvenir of the great strike!'

146

THEATRES IN STRIKE TIME.

All the plays which had previously shown themselves to be 'good lives' have managed to live on through the last ten days, and some of them report fairly good business. There were enough people staying in the centre of town at night to make the nucleus of an audience, and it was, no doubt, to catch this public that Mr. Playfair's revue 'Riverside Nights' was brought up from Hammersmith to the Ambassadors Theatre.

Mr. Fagan bravely proposed to hold the first night of 'The Plough and the Stars,' Mr. O'Casey's new piece, on Wednesday. His courage was rewarded, for the strike was called off at midday, and taxis were about in small numbers by the evening. The usual first-night audience arrived, but their usual unpunctuality was of no account, since some of the scenery had been on strike and could only be got back to work after a delay. Mr. Augustus John, a rare first-nighter, was one of a company which gave Mr. O'Casey a tremendous reception and drew from him a neat little speech.

Evening dress was rare, and it was odd to be at an important theatrical occasion where people sat in the stalls in grey suits, deeply studying country newspapers of whose existence they had scarcely been aware before.

p.2

AN EXPLANATION.
Manchester Newspapers Still Held Up.

As the general strike was 'called off' on Wednesday afternoon some explanation is naturally demanded for the non-appearance of the ordinary editions of the 'Manchester Guardian' and 'Evening News.' Briefly stated, the present position of the newspaper press is this:—

Newspaper production, brought to a standstill by the general strike, is completely disorganised, and the prospects for the immediate future are uncertain. Newspaper proprietors are therefore unable to guarantee employment at once to all their workers on the terms of the old contracts broken when the strike began, but the Manchester newspaper proprietors have expressed their willingness to re-engage their full staffs on a day-to-day contract, reserving the right to make reductions in the number employed if circumstances compel them to do so.

An agreement embodying these provisions and also a guarantee against all recrimination or vindictiveness was drawn up and discussed with local representatives of the various trade unions concerned in newspaper printing and publication and was on the point of being signed when the representatives of the

Typographical Association were instructed by their Executive Council to refuse to accept any terms except full reinstatement of all strikers on the old terms, including engagement terminable only on a fortnight's notice.

In view of the serious financial losses already sustained and the uncertainty of the present position it was impossible for the newspaper owners to accept this demand, which would have involved the necessity of continuing to pay the members of the staff even though the publication of the paper had for any reason been once more suddenly made impossible.

Normal newspaper production is therefore at present impossible.

Terms Offered to the Men.

The following are the terms which were offered for resumption of work by the Manchester Guardian and Evening News, Limited, and Allied Newspapers, Limited:–

1. All employees who return to work do so on the conditions and agreements which were in force prior to the dispute, but on a day-to-day engagement, pending any national settlement by the various unions affected. The day-to-day agreement to be reviewed at the end of a fortnight.

2. Experimentally the proprietors are prepared to reinstate all regular men at once, but in view of the unsettled conditions are at liberty to reduce staffs as may be deemed necessary.

3. No new labour will be introduced in the meanwhile.

4. Both sides to agree, as far as lies in their power, to support the policy that there shall be no victimisation in respect of any action taken during the stoppage.

THE MERRY MONTH!

(Lines respectfully dedicated to the Poor Public, by a sympathiser.)

If you thought you'd be in clover
    When the general strike was done
Lo, the general strike is over
    And the work is unbegun;
You have swapped your earlier tangle
    For a burden hardly lesser,
And a good old general wrangle
    Is the general strike's successor.

Still the meetings are in session,
    Still 'developments' arise;
And another, 'deep depression'

Sails along from Iceland's skies.
Oh, confound May altogether–
    One development I'd like
Is a stoppage of this weather
    And to see the rain on strike!

LUCIO.

In a Government message broadcast yesterday it was suggested that employers dispensing without notice with the services of any paid volunteer should follow the practice which the Government propose to pursue and grant a gratuity of at least two days' pay.

Saturday May 15 1926   *p.7*

THROUGH U.S. EYES.
Mr. Baldwin's Personal Triumph.

(From our own Correspondent.)

New York, Friday.

American press comment and public opinion, as judged by the financial market, remain cautious in estimating the effects of the British strike settlement. Only the 'Times' and 'Evening Post' (New York) see it as a demonstration of the failure of the general strike as a weapon. Other newspapers frankly express doubt where substantial victory lies, save with the British nation itself. Every editor speaks of the basic sanity of the people which triumphed finally. The Hearst press, asserting that the British learn only under compulsion, believe they have learned moderation in handling labour disputes. It is suspected here that Mr. Baldwin for diplomatic reasons neglected to expose the fact that Labour leaders called off the strike because it was a complete debacle. Throughout the press the Premier is hailed as a great constitutional hero and the only personal victor in the crisis.

MISCELLANY

WHEN THE NEWS REACHED MANCHESTER.

Whatever unforeseen litter might remain to be cleared up – or created – there was no doubt about the mood of most people in the early afternoon of Wednesday when the news came through that the general strike was 'off.' It was one of simple and uncalculating relief – the mood of thankfulness for the lifting of a great shadow. It was the mood when barriers break down, when no men are strangers in their immediate grasp of good news. In Manchester streets men's faces had the look which one observer said he had not seen since the morning of November 11, 1918: one passer-by would say to another, 'Heard the news?' and, seeing that news written on his neighbour's face, would pass on with a glance and a laugh. Into one private car, driving into Manchester and held up for a second in the traffic at the corner of Cross Street and Albert Square, the head and shoulders of a complete stranger with a stiff grey moustache and gleaming blue eye were suddenly thrust. 'Na poo – fini!' said their owner to the driver and his companion, and withdrew as swiftly as he had appeared. If the thing was not 'na-poo-ed' and finished quite so cleanly and quickly as most hearers of the T.U.C. withdrawal then imagined it would be, the delay was not for lack of either relief or goodwill on the part of most individual inhabitants of this country.

AS SEEN BY OTHERS.

On the whole our general strike enjoyed what might be called 'a good press.' Naturally, in this sense of the term the press had to be the foreign press, for our own was a little too deeply implicated in the general disaster to be capable of stepping back and taking a detached view of the production. But the French and American papers seem to have been united in their admiration of the steadiness and lack of disorder with which a normally highly organised country faces up to a very highly organised stoppage. As if to underline the compliments and give us further support in our ordeal there was the news of the mere Joan of Arc celebration in Paris on Sunday last, a festival in honour of which admirers and detesters of what St. Joan has been made to stand for in French politics managed to provide more police casualties in one afternoon than were apparently achieved in the whole of the eight days of our own national stoppage.

THE HOSTILE NOTE.

The only grumbling or dissentient note in the favourable criticisms of the foreign experts on Labour's big push was supplied by the German correspondents who, according to the 'British Gazette,' 'have a very poor opinion of the ability of the British trade unions to carry out a general strike and maintain that even the youngest [presumably German] students of revolutionary technique could 'have shown the Labour leader how to do their work better.' There seems to be here some slight misapprehension of the nature of the production staged by the T.U.C. It was, after all, a general strike and not an armed revolution. And as a general strike it had the air, to those who were in the middle of it, of a pretty effective piece of work. 'Made in Germany' it might have been produced with more bloodshed, but that is to overlook the fact that there is a slight difference between a strike and a battle. It is, perhaps, an odd thing to be proud of, but one is inclined to 'Support British Industries' to the extent of an assurance that even in the strike industry the home-made article is better value in the long run.

EYES AND NO EYES.

Few items of strike news in Manchester did more to keep the public smiling in a time of crisis than the assurance from the "British Worker" that in the matter of street traffic the place was 'like a deserted city.' If Manchester's traffic during the strike was that of a deserted city most people would not like to encounter a really congested area. The odd thing is that the paper which published this extraordinary view of the situation on the roads was actually printed in Manchester; a mere walk out of the office would have convinced its editor-in-charge that his report of the death of traffic was, in Mark Twain's phrase, greatly exaggerated. Even the lorries were nothing like so rare in the steady jam of wheeled vehicles as the writer of this obituary notice announced. 'I walked three miles this morning,' he wrote, 'and saw three.' He might have stood still for ten minutes and counted thirty. If he had been moderately lucky he might even have beheld one of the most engaging of the lot. This was seen driving earnestly up the Oxford Road bearing a cargo of barrels of beer. And the legend at the side of the driver's head ran:– 'FOOD - URGENT.'

THE ROAD WALKERS.

Another news item which deserves a fairly high place among the brighter sort was the announcement given out by the broadcasting people towards the end of last week that 'The National Road Walking Championship arranged to be held at St. Albans on Saturday next has been postponed.' It was felt by many listeners that this was pure petulance on the part of St. Albans. The National Road Walking Championship was at last being staged on a really national scale; it seemed no reason why St. Albans should drop out of the celebration in a fit of merely parochial pique.

'JUST LIKE SALFORD.'

There may have been some deep question of policy concerned in the delay in restarting the Salford trams, but both the Tramways Committee and the tramway workers of that newly created city may be interested to learn that that was not at all how it seemed to strike a good many of their fellow-citizens. Casual conversation with several of those citizens on roads that were on Thursday still unsupplied with a tram service revealed a surprising unanimity of comment. It was crystallised in the cheery assurance of a working man on foot – 'Just like Salford – always behind everybody else.' Salford a city – but still Salford, apparently. As a matter of fact, amid the distractions and rumours of Thursday there seemed to be a certain underlying moral in the attitude of cheerful contempt adopted by the citizens towards the continued absence of their tram service – the moral that if any body of masters or men (or both) chose to proceed on the assumption that the great strike had been called off in order that a lot of little strikes might begin they need not expect to receive any warm tributes to their commonsense from the public at large.

PAST PRAYING FOR.

It is to be hoped that James – aged 2½ – has been duly informed by this time of the T.U.C. decision and of the settlement of many subsidiary difficulties. For on Tuesday night last 'miscellany' is assured that James was taking a very intransigent line 'Say your prayers, darling,' was his mother's suggestion. 'No prayers to-night Mummie,' said James firmly. 'Not till the Strike's over.'

SEATS OF THE MIGHTY.

(Any passenger to any tramguard.)

If, guard, as I tender my penny
    My air should be distant and chill,
You need not assume it is any
    Particular sign of ill-will.
I am glad you are back on your platform—
    Though I think you were rather an ass,
Any feelings that tend to take that form
    Will very soon pass.

But, Herbert, I feel a bit haughty;
    For, Herbert (if such be your name)
While you have been forward and naughty
    I've scored at least once in the game;
For rides that my means had forbidden
    At last I've been free to afford –
For sixpence, dear Herbert, I've ridden
    To town like a lord.

For that not too exorbitant sum down
    In seats of the mighty I've sat –
And a tram seems a bit of a come-down
    To one who has travelled like that,
I hated the strike and its manner,
    The news of its ending was bliss–
But those taxicab rides for a tanner
    I really *shall* miss.

                              LUCIO.

It was announced yesterday that the Emergency Regulations would continue in full force and would not be relaxed until there had been a general return to work.

p.6

OUR LONDON CORRESPONDENCE

By Private Wire.

London, Friday Night.

THE SECOND DAY MOOD.

To those who are not emotionally interested in the simple football match question of who has won, and who are really interested in what effect the general strike and its consequences have had on our political and industrial history to-day and the next few days will be days of documents. The day before yesterday there was a formal surrender on the part of the trade unions. Yesterday it was Mafficking Night among the employers, as Mr. Baldwin not obscurely hinted in the House of Commons. To-day it is the realities of the accommodation.

The general strike has come and gone, perhaps for ever. The unions yesterday stayed out because they declined unconditional surrender. Last night and to-day both employers and employed have been at work on conditions. The railway companies and the railwaymen have been the first big organisations to agree. The

153

terms of agreement are printed in another column. At the first glance they look as if the railwaymen have passed under the yoke. It is not really quite so. The railwaymen are to be taken on at their old wages and their old positions as fast as the railway companies can resume work. There is no mention of keeping on men who volunteered during the strike and who would like to continue the work. Probably that is a small element. But the railway companies have not thought it worth while to make a point of it. I understand also that the railway companies have agreed to pay the men the back pay – that is, the pay due to them for about a week before the strike began, which legally the railway companies were entitled to retain on the ground of breach of contract. This was one of the chief things that was holding back the railway settlement to-day.

Much more important is that the Prime Minister has taken an entirely new step and decided to propose for the first time the terms that the Government think ought to be accepted by the miners and mineowners. If the general strike was intended to force the Government to take the initiative not as an intermediary but as an inventor of solutions, then the general strike has succeeded. Of course it has not succeeded. If it had never happened the Government would eventually have reached that stage. For good or evil the necessity of the government's intervention, and in the last resort its decision seems now to be accepted.

THE COURT IN THE STRIKE.

The King came to London during the strike, but this time did not visit the Hyde Park camp, as he did during the railway strike. The Prince of Wales, who flew over from France at the beginning, visited Paddington one morning to see the undergraduates doing drill with the milk cans. The Duke of York visited Hyde Park.

An event in the ornamental life of London that the strike brought about was that the King's Life Guards mounted only one day in khaki, and on that day the 'boxes' at the Horse Guards were closed, so the famous mounted sentries there were not seen except in full dress.

The Household Cavalry were used to a considerable extent for protection and police duties, and it is likely that the regiments in London may occupy Hyde Park instead of Regent's Park barracks. In the present case the Blues were brought from Windsor to Hyde Park barracks. All regiments at Hyde Park can reach Parliament and the palace by park all the way except the crossing at Hyde Park Corner, and from there can move quickly.

A STRIKE STORY.

One night a Government official went out into the East End to find two policemen who were wanted for some purpose. He

154

inquired in a public-house which was full of strikers. A striker said he knew where the policemen were, and would tell him if he would buy a copy of the 'British Worker.' The official did so. The striker then said that he must read the leading article first, which he did.

The official was then conveyed to a back room, where the two policemen were discovered peacefully resting from their activities. Police and strikers were on the best of terms and in harmonious possessions of their allotted territories.

WASTED DAYS.

The great majority of Londoners will write off the ten days of the general strike and the two days that have followed as a period that has slipped from their practical life. The display of energy on the part of hundreds of thousands of people has been terrific, but it could not lead to much. The men and women who valiantly tramped to their places of business day after day found little to do when they arrived, for customers were few and the crowds who thronged the pavements and gazed in at shop windows were, like most of us, merely putting off time. It was to while away the time quite as much as the idea that if one waited long enough exciting incidents would be seen that kept the strikers and their women folk hanging about in the streets in the neighbourhood of storm centres.

The people who stayed at home and made plans to spend their leisure profitably doing some serious reading and writing or carrying out some work in the house or garden that they had been longing to do found that they could not settle to anything. When asked by their friends how they were employing themselves they would say enthusiastically, 'Oh, I have a lot of jobs to do.' Asked if they were doing them, they would say, after cogitation, 'No, I don't seem able to!' In many homes the B.B.C. made definite work impossible, for the thought of the past announcement and the coming news was always on the mind.

DIPLOMACY IN THE STRIKE.

By a fortunate coincidence there were no big movements afoot in world diplomacy during the strike. So far as the British Foreign Office was concerned, the only business on hand was the sitting of the League Committees at Geneva, and the only practical effect of the strike was that Lord Cecil last Saturday flew as far as Paris. From Paris he went to Geneva by train.

The Ambassadors and Ministers have called at the Foreign Office as usual on routine matters, their main concern being to collect material for reports on the situation here. Some of the foreign diplomats have a comparative background for their observation of the British so-called but miscalled 'general strike,' and those who have were inclined to regard it as child's play. The Germans, for instance, simply say there has been no such thing as a general strike here. In Germany there was no gas or electricity, no telephone, no telegrams, no communication – a complete smash, ruining everybody without distinction.

The T.U.C. could not have organised or conducted the strike without the telephone and telegraph, yet it was the telephone and the telegraph that enabled the government to fight the strike. The bank staffs could not be called out, because the banks were as necessary to the T.U.C. as to anybody else. The Stock Exchange was more immediately necessary to the T.U.C. than to so-called capitalists, because about £3,000,000 worth of securities had to be realised for strike pay. Food and medical supplies are necessary without distinction of persons.

In short, a really general strike (as opposed to the partial strike just over) is impossible, because by the nature of things it cannot be organised without bringing immediate ruin to the organisers.

'THE BRITISH GAZETTE.'

'The British Gazette' published its last issue yesterday. The Government has got no credit out of it. From the beginning it has been run as a silly propaganda sheet. The only result of all that has been that no reader of all its millions has felt able to trust even its perfectly accurate statements of fact, because in every column of the paper there have been signs of bias and propaganda. It might have served a purpose. A dry statement of news received might have won confidence and was what everybody, even the simplest, desired in the conditions of things created by the trade unions' suppression of the press.

Several very bad instances of uncritical partisanship have been noted in Parliament. Perhaps the worst offence of the 'British Gazette' was its reports of Parliament. It chose to give a highly coloured 'sketch' of a militant kind when what people wanted was a faithful report of what took place in Parliament. Even an impartial precis in the space devoted by the 'British Gazette' to Parliament would have been worth something, and the 'British Gazette' had space enough and paper enough to have given a three or four columns report. Parliament was the centre of news.

A full and fair report of Parliament was the only kind of news that in the atmosphere of the general strike the public were in the least prepared to believe. The 'British Gazette' failed in that in a way that day by day embarrassed conscientious journalists with a sympathetic shame.

156

This morning for the first time the announcer at the B.B.C. said that he had nothing to announce. This cheered people with hopes of things getting right again. But for a thinning out of the motor traffic in the morning the look of London during the day has been very much the same as at any time during the strike.

The printers were not back, and there was the same outcrop of queer little sheets in the streets, and the hawkers bore up wonderfully, and occasionally, from sheer force of habit, shouted 'All the winners.' To-day two of the evening papers managed to bring out four-page issues in print, and what restored confidence as much as anything was that one of them had a cross-word puzzle containing a few topical problems.

Our strike good humour, which has staggered the world, continues, and it was specially pleasing in the Tubes, where undergraduate courtesy was a nice change from the curt severity of the normal staff. The 'buses were still run in a spirit of adventure. One was seen with a hole in the wire-netting over which there was a notice: 'This is where to throw the bricks.' Private cars were still giving people lifts at the busy hours.

Milk control is continuing till next Monday, and Hyde Park is still closed. When it is over one of the biggest jobs will be the resorting of milk churns now scattered all over the country. When the Hyde Park milk shop is in full blast they are handling there about 20,000 churns and over 200,000 gallons of milk a day.

p.7

HOW THE B.B.C. CARRIED ON

The end of the strike means the end of a period of great strain at the Savoy Hill headquarters of the B.B.C. The first effect of the crisis was to throw a highly complicated mechanism somewhat out of gear. Programmes were disorganised, but almost the whole staff of the B.B.C. was quickly reorganised in such a way as to relieve the departments where the work was heaviest. Many officials were either housed on the premises or slept at adjourning hotels.

The burden upon the announcers soon became so heavy that the usual staff was unequal to it, and officials, including Mr. Reith, managing director, Admiral Carpendale, controller, and Captain Eckersley, chief engineer, gave assistance. Soon it became necessary to organise a special department to classify the news which was continually flowing in and prepare it for the announcers. Before long there were a dozen officials at work in this department.

157

Throughout the trouble Mr. Reith was in consultation with Mr. Davidson, the Deputy Chief Civil Commissioner, and spent part of his time at the latter's headquarters at the Admiralty. Every item of news was read to Mr. Reith before being broadcast. The building was under police protection but there was no attempt at interference. Mr. Baldwin's broadcast on Saturday night took place from 10, Downing Street, a microphone being specially installed for the purpose.

The role of the BBC throughout the strike was bitterly resented by the trade unions, who saw the Corporation as acting purely as a mouthpiece for the Government.

p.6

Leader   **SETTLING DOWN.**

The second day after the general strike has been a great improvement on the first. The agreement reached on the railways is a considerable achievement, and should do much to facilitate a resumption of work in all other directions. So long as the railwaymen remained out it was impossible for employers to gauge their position, or in many cases, to bind themselves to the reinstatement of their full staffs. With that great cause of uncertainty removed resumption of work should now be rapid and general. The terms of the railway settlement are probably unique in the history of British labour disputes. That is perhaps natural, since the dispute itself was of an entirely novel kind and beyond the legitimate scope of trade unionism. It may well be that the judgment of the High Court that those who took part in it were acting illegally and had no protection at law under the Trade Disputes Act had a good deal to do with the submission of the three railway unions to terms which amount not merely to defeat but to public confession of wrong doing. In substance the railwaymen do not lose much. There is to be no interference with rates of pay or conditions of work, and men will be taken on by seniority as work can be found for them to do. On the other hand the formal admission of guilt is unreserved. Moreover, it is coupled with the recognition of the companies' legal right to claim damages for breach of contract, with a solemn undertaking not to repeat the offence, with consent to the transfer of individuals (without loss of pay) to, presumably, inferior positions, and with the dismissal of those who have been guilty of violence or intimidation. Provided that action under this last clause is confined to cases proved in a court of law the terms seem not unreasonable, if they are reasonably interpreted by the companies.

With this formal admission by the railwaymen of 'a wrongful act' we may reasonably hope to have seen the last of the lightning strike in responsibly organised trade unions. And if the lightning strike is out of the way the general strike loses much of such attraction as it may once have had for the hotheads of the Labour movement. It will be a long time, at least, before the country is again held up by the threat of general industrial paralysis. That is a considerable time to set against the havoc wrought in the last fortnight. But is that all that is likely to emerge? It is too soon to say, but upheavals on this scale often set an unexpected ferment at work. In this case one may hazard the guess that there may be a new way of looking at some of the underlying problems of trade unionism and its relation to the State. The general strike was as certainly in fact as it is said not to have been in intention a threat to democratic government. In other words, the trade unions, or some of them, have attained a degree of power which, misdirected, threatens our constitutional liberties – freedom of opinion, freedom of Parliament, and even freedom to work. For the time being the threat has been repelled, and it may be several years before the trade unions recover the moral and material losses which they have incurred in the last few days. Nevertheless the problem would be likely in time to recur, for it is inherent in the existing method of trade union organisation. Is it not possible that, just as the Great War directed men's minds to new methods of securing international peace, through the League fo Nations, they may after this internal conflict seek new methods of securing industrial peace?

There seem to be three choices. The first and easiest would be to let things take their course. In that case the next few months would be likely to see much hard bargaining intended to take advantage of the present exhaustion of the trade unions and to get depressed industries on their legs at the expense of wages. whatever adjustments of this kind may be necessary would bring no final solution of the problem. The second would be voluntary reorganisation by the trade unions, or at least a change of method which would divert the greater part of their energies from strikes to equipping themselves to take a more responsible part in the direction of industry. That can only be left to them to decide. The third, and perhaps most hopeful, lies in Parliamentary action. But there is danger even here. Crude legislation to provide an effective strike-breaking organisation, or to cripple the political activities of the unions or to deprive them, without compensation, of the protection of the Trade Disputes Act, or to impose new penalties for new offences in the conduct of strikes would merely be provocative of the class war which is, at bottom, the very danger to be guarded against. On the other hand, the problem of strikes on the railways and other essential services is one which can probably only be dealt with by the State, perhaps by direct prohibition. But it should be obvious that the services from which the right to strike was withdrawn should be compensated liberally in other ways – by security of employment, by the right of appeal to independent arbitral authority, by pensions and in other ways. The collapse of the general strike and the new ideas on the legitimate functions of the trade unions to which it has given rise make the present an admirable occasion for considering whether it is not possible to give a happier turn to the prevailing and somewhat anarchic relations between the trade unions and the rest of the community.

p.7

BACK TO COAL DISCUSSION.
Premier's Move.

WHAT THE INDUSTRY IS OFFERED.
Plan Compared with Samuel Scheme.

(From our Labour Correspondent.)

London, Friday.

After two months of fruitless negotiations in the coal industry punctuated by a general strike and ending in a national coal stoppage, the Prime Minister has decided that the coalowners and miners cannot be expected to come to terms and that the Government must propound what it considers a 'reasonable basis' for the settlement of the dispute on the lines of the Commission's report. The proposals were handed to the coalowners and miners to-night, and will be considered to-day.

They will be liked by neither side – which is probably in their favour – and are less favourable to the miners than the Samuel Memorandum. They are less far-reaching than the Commission's report itself, for Mr. Baldwin does not include in his programme (whether finally, one does not know) nationalisation of royalties and the setting up of a Coal Commission to administer the national mineral property and the granting of powers to municipalities for the distribution of coal.

A subsidy is granted but in strictly limited form; three millions is to suffice to meet all the needs of the transition period, except that some undefined sum will be allowed for the assistance of men displaced from closed pits. The text of the proposals rivals in calculated vagueness the famous wages chapter of the Commission's report. The vagueness may, however, be merely a prelude and a spur to negotiation.

The essentials of the proposals are firstly, a legislative and administrative programme, which the Government will 'introduce and endeavour to pass this session.' This involves the passing of

160

bills for facilitating amalgamations, laying a welfare levy on royalty owners, restricting recruitment in mines, and setting up a National Wages Board for the coal industry. There are to be set up

A National Fuel and Power Council:

A committee to promote the adoption of larger mineral waggons on railways and greater concentration of ownerhsip of waggons;

A committee to investigate the question of coal selling syndicates (co-operative selling);

A committee to examine the Commission's suggestions for compulsory profit-sharing and a family allowance system;

A committee on housing in colliery districts.

There is to be prepared, perhaps by other committees, a scheme for the establishment of pit committees and plans for the asistance of men displaced from pits.

Before any of these steps is taken a full statement must be laid before a Coal Advisory Committee. Of this committee we are told nothing now. It is presumably that which the Government suggested on April 30, on which miners and owners would be represented to advise the Mines Department as to the steps that can be taken to put into operation: 'whatever proposals or reorganisation are of benefit to the industry.'

The Interim Period.

The second section of the proposals relates to the interim period during which the industry is to frame a national wages and hours agreement. Much of the controversy in the abortive negotiations turned on the length of the period and the amount the Government should give to make up wages until a new basis is fixed. The Samuel Memorandum suggested a 'reasonable period,' which the miners think should be two or three months, during which wages should be continued at present rates. The Government propoals propose in effect an immediate reduction in the minimum percentage of an amount and for a period of weeks to be determined by agreement. During this period owners should forego (as a whole though not necessarily individually) profits, and the Government should 'fill the gap with a subsidy to be debited against the £3,000,000 aforesaid.' With present prices and costs of production it is almost inevitable that this should involve immediate wages reduction and surrender of profits, as at the present rate the whole subsidy would last for less than six weeks.

'In the meantime' there is to be set up a Wages Board of three owners and three miners' representatives with an independent chairman, to frame a national wages and hours agreement. It is not, however, clear whether this board is the 'National Wages Board on the lines of the Railway Wages Board' which is to be set up by statutory authority. The Railway Board is a bigger body, six a-side, with four representatives of outside interests and an independent chairman. Sir Herbert Samuel also suggested the addition of 'a neutral element' to any coal board. But whether it is the final statutory body or a temporary body, a wages board is to be set up 'to issue a decision within three weeks' on the form of the national agreement and the wages to be paid.

The Wage Question.

The clause defining the principles on which wages shall be determined is vague on the crucial point of district minima. One may read it as one pleases. The national agreement is to govern the principles 'on which the general wage rates should be ascertained in each district,' and the Board is to 'decide the minimum percentage on basis, taking into consideration the state and prospects of trade, the reorganisation proposals of the Commission, and other relevant factors.' Some authorities to-night see in this scope to fix minima for each district, others hold that one national percentage is contemplated.

There is to be a low cash national minimum subsistence. Wages are not to fall below 45s. in a full week – the Lancashire figure, which the Commission took 'as fairly representing the lowest adult wage for a full week's work over any large district.' The Board is to fix the districts. Most important of all, 'in the event of disagreement in respect of wages the decision shall rest with the independent chairman.'

The Government adds two clauses to these proposals – one offering immediate legislation if the parties agree that some 'temporary modification' of the Seven Hours' Act should be made; the other providing for the application of any balance of the three millions left over after the interim period as a 'tapering subsidy.' The 'provisional undertakings made by the Government in this memorandum are conditional on the acceptance of its terms by the other parties.'

Mr. Baldwin does not expect an answer to his proposals before Monday, but he will hardly get it so early. The Mining Association, I hear, will probably desire to consult its district associations. The miners' conference to-morrow may refer the proposals back to the districts. The wages reduction proposals will be difficult for them to accept after their previous declarations.

Mr. MacDonald's Comment.

In a comment to-night Mr. Ramsay MacDonald, while not endorsing the proposals, said that 'if the Government had produced them three weeks ago there would have been no strike.' Whether Mr. MacDonald is right in his judgment or not I think it is true to say that in essentials these proposals were in Mr. Baldwin's possession on April 30 when the break came that led to the general strike decision. Certainly on that day he had fully decided that the government must at an early date state its own idea of terms, and he had in mind £3,000,000 as the limit of financial assistance. Why he kept the terms up his sleeve must remain an unsolved problem.

As might have been expected, Baldwin's offer of mediation was unacceptable to both the owners and the miners. The decision to omit several of the key features of long-term reorganisation contained in the Samuel Report led the miners to refuse to negotiate on immediate pay cuts while the owners, operating from a position of strength, were intent on holding out for nothing less than a major reduction in wages and an increase in hours.

Monday May 17 1926   *p.7*

WHY THE STRIKE WAS CALLED OFF.
The T.U.C.'s Perilous Choice.

RISKS OF CALLING OUT THE 'SECOND LINE.'
Letting Loose Revolutionary Forces.

SAMUEL MEMORANDUM'S APPEAL TO A HARASSED COUNCIL.

(From our Labour Correspondent.)

London, Sunday.

The general strike is now a matter of history. Its effects on the Labour movement will not be seen for some time. It is too soon to measure its influence on the course of the coal negotiations, to say how far the breach between the General Council and the miners is momentary, and to judge whether the strike will strengthen the trade unions of the Right and throw the movement back on the old-fashioned methods, or whether it will strengthen the Left-wing ideas and give impetus to the Communist theory of mass sympathetic action. But it is perhaps worth while now to analyse some of the events of the last fortnight. In Friday's 'Manchester Guardian' some account was given of the inner history of the nine days of the strike and in particular of the division between the General Council and the miners which has led to sharp recrimination and a feeling that the miners were 'let down' by their allies. One may now relate this history as it appears from the point of view of the General Council.

In the first place one must emphasise that there was no shred of revolutionary sentiment in the inception of the strike. When the General Council announced and repeated daily that it was engaged on a purely industrial struggle, that no attack on the

163

Constitution was intended, and that it did not visualise a political victory, it meant what it said. The thoroughness of the attack on the vital services of the country, the offer to take over food distribution and to supply power were, in fact, challenges of the right of the political State to maintain the life of society. But the first was viewed by the Council merely as an ordinary industrial stoppage; the second was a gesture to prove to the public that although its business was to be crippled there was no wish to starve it. The position was illogical, but the General Council had not thought out, and certainly did not intend to carry out the logical implications of its actions.

The Germ of the Strike.

The initial blunder was to have embarked on a general strike at all. But here there was no deep-laid or carefully prepared plan. The strike was seen as a defensive action against the mineowers, which unfortunately became an attack on the Government because the Government could not secure the lifting of lock-out notices. The germ of the strike was the assistance the transport unions could render to the miners by refusing to handle coal. This was extended to embrace the printing and heavy industries because, first, the bigger the movement the more were thought to be the chances of peace, and, second, the transport unions were a little reluctant to bear the brunt of trouble and urged that if there were risks they should not be the only ones to bear them.

But until the eleventh hour before the strike began perhaps none of the leaders believed in his heart that it would come. The margins of discussion were so narrow, the consequences so great, that throughout the week-end Mr. Thomas and his colleagues felt that somehow a bargain with the Government might be struck. A few more hours' talk on the Friday night, a few more hours' talk on the Sunday night, and the appropriate face-saving formula might have been found. Perhaps if the miners had not gone home to their districts, if Mr. Baldwin had stayed out of bed half an hour longer on Monday morning, or if the Birkenhead formula had become a real bargaining instrument instead of a piece of paper left on the Cabinet table, the general strike would have been averted. But the Government made its choice for war and called the bluff which without much heart the General Council was putting up. The 'Daily Mail' incident was used to closure discussions. The strike therefore began.

General Council's Policy.

The issues at stake were never clear, and the General Council held that they were fighting only to secure a basis of negotiation on which miners, owners, and Government could meet with promise that the miners would not be utterly crushed. In spite of its consistent public support of the miners the General Council had never shared the miners' view of wages. From the beginning it sought to persuade the miners to accept the Commission's report in the sense of taking a temporary reduction for the higher paid men as the price of a well-assured and far-reaching scheme of reorganisation. A little plain speaking on April 8 led the miners on the following day to tie their executive's hands by the resolution against any wages reductions that has proved so serious a stumbling block. The Council worked hard to overcome this obstacle and to bring the miners and the Government to face the report, but the miners would not move and Mr. Baldwin, faced by Cabinet difficulties and the mineowners' extreme demands, would not take a bold line. He lamented the stubbornness of miners and owners, he toyed with ideas but could not declare the Government's mind. Had he made his proposals of May 14 on April 30, or even had he secured the withdrawal of notices on April 30, the Council would have been able to continue its pressure on the miners with some hope of success.

T.U.C.'s Peace Efforts.

The first few days of the strike produced a hardening of tempers but the Council can fairly urge that it lost no time in trying to get the strike over on fair terms. It responded sympathetically, after its first shyness, to mediation efforts. It embraced the Archbishop's plan, and it carrried on with energy its conversations with Sir Herbert Samuel and other mediators whose part is not so widely known. In these the miners took no substantial part. On Monday and Tuesday of last week the Council had the Samuel proposals and discussed them at length with the miners. At one point the Council thought that the miners had accepted them as a basis of negotiation, and hoped that with this joint acceptance, and in the belief that the Government was not unfavourable, it might be possible so to arrange matters that if the strike were called off the government would be able almost immediately to respond by getting lock-out notices withdrawn and negotiations started on the Samuel basis.

Sometime on Tuesday the miners appear to have changed their minds and declared their rejection of the Samuel proposals as a means of calling off the strike, while stating their willingness to submit this to a delegate conference. (There is conflict on this point, but I am here recording the General Council's impression.) Late on Tuesday night, or rather in the small hours of Wednesday morning, the Council took its decision to go to Mr. Baldwin with the Samuel memorandum and call off the strike, leaving the miners to negotiate alone on the improved terms which the memorandum offered.

Letting Loose Revolutionary Forces.

The motives for this course are most difficult to disentangle. They were not simple. One doubts if any member of the General

Council would care to sum them up in a sentence. The explanations one can offer are not discreditable to the good sense of the Council, however they may reflect on its consistency and courage as strike organisers.

1. The strike had reached a critical stage. It was unbroken – no sections were pressing to return to work. The 'first line' had, however, been called up, and the Government had overcome some of the first effects. The engineers and shipbuilding trade, although only called out on the Tuesday, were reckoned as part of the 'first line.' Their response was not good, but the problem most urgently before the Council was the extension of the strike to the second line – the electrical power men and gas-workers and the Post Office employees. The power men were restive, the Council's attempt to come to terms with local authorities was not proving successful.

But the consequences of such extension, the Council felt, would be extraordinarily grave. The challenge to the Government of a cutting off of light and power and a cessation of the postal, telephone, and telegraph services would be unmistakable. However little the Council desired it, revolutionary forces would be let loose. The industrial centres would be cut off from the centre, each strike committee would become in effect a soviet.

Ominous Signs.

2. Government action seemed to be intensifying – an embargo had been placed on the receipt of foreign aid, however unrevolutionary the helpers, the paper supplies of the 'British Worker' had been interfered with and its office raided, a phrase of the Attorney General seemed to presage direct action against the Council. The Astbury judgment, the speech of Sir John Simon, and the Government's pledge to maintain the trade union rights of non-strikers and blacklegs were ominous signs. The protected food convoys, the armoured cars and tanks in the London streets, the armed cordon, round the docks, the new constabulary force all seemed to make for civil trouble and conflict with authority and rendered an extension, or even the continuance of the strike, highly perilous to the order with which it had so far been conducted. By the end of the week the pinch of desperation might begin to be felt and a drift back to work began which on the analogy of earlier strikes, might prove an incentive to disorder.

Resentment and Tiredness.

(3) There was a feeling of resentment at the miners' obstinacy. Although the workers of the country had made so great a sacrifice on their behalf the miners seemed to respond so little to all efforts at compromise.

(4) Much weight must be given to the effect on the General Council of the strain of weeks of negotiations, meetings night after

night until the small hours, prolonged argument and controversy, combined now with the responsibility of organising a great strike movement with hastily improvised machinery. Some of the negotiators, like Mr. Thomas, added Parliamentary duties; all had their own trade union work to fit in. The General Council was the very opposite of a revolutionary committee of action. It was a body of tired trade union officials living in an unhealthy smoke laden atmosphere, suffering from lack of sleep, wearied of wrangling with miners and Cabinet Ministers and insistent deputations of strikers, worried by fears of disorder, subject (in the absence of a public press) to panic rumours in remote touch with the great industrial centres, and anxious, above all things, that the situation should not pass out of control.

On the one side there was the pressure of the Parliamentary Labour party naturally timid for its future, on the other was the Left wing and the Communists, happily so far prevented (by the press embargo) from the dissemination of a conscious strike philosophy but pressing to go ahead.

The Samuel Memorandum.

5. To this body of trade union secretaries and officials the Samuel memorandum seemed to offer three solid advantages. It assured the miners against an immediate reduction of wages, it took wages out of the hands of the mineowners and miners and put them under a National Wages Board stabilised by a neutral element, it promised reorganisation and made reorganisation the condition of wages revision. Further, the memorandum appeared to have the tacit, if not explicit, approval of the Government.

Controversy will long turn on the sufficiency of these reasons. The final decision was taken swiftly. Labour critics will ask why the Council did not wait another day and try once more to carry the miners with them or to secure acceptance of the Samuel memorandum as a pledge against victimisation from the Government. The only answer seems to be that the Council determined to cut its losses at all costs and trusting that the boldness of the decision would work in its favour.

THE STRIKE MADE INEVITABLE.
Mr. MacDonald's View.

BLAME PLACED ON THE CABINET.
Was it a Success?

Mr. J. Ramsay MacDonald, speaking at Shepherd's Bush last night, on behalf of the Labour candidate in the Hammersmith North by-election, said the Government candidate was attempting to make tremendous capital out of the general strike, and in order to do so was treating it with somewhat the same frame of mind as that with which the Zinovieff letter was treated.

'They tell you that it was a revolution,' said Mr. MacDonald. 'They tell you it was a deliberate attack and challenge to the ordinary working of the Constitution. They tell you that you all came out not to support the miners but in obedience to some sinister and devilish call from a foreign country to upset your own. And unfortunately a good many people believe in that nonsense. You know and I know it was nothing of the kind. You know and I know that that extraordinary manifestation of human solidarity was an extraordinary manifestation that men and women nowadays cannot stand idly by whilst millions of their own flesh and blood are going to be ground down in their standard of life, and it was that sentiment and that sentiment alone which brought three million men out.

No Political Issues.

'Whatever we may think of the general strike, either as an industrial or political weapon, in any event we should not tell lies about it. My position is perfectly well known. In these last days – I know what I am talking about and I do not require to read the "British Gazette" to be put into possession of the facts – what happened was this. By the way the Government handled the negotiations by the way they neglected their opportunities, by the way they declined to follow the path of reason, by the way they turned a deaf ear and a blind eye to every approach to common sense and good sense, by the end of that week they had "boxed" the whole of the trade union movement until there was one thing and one thing only they could do as a united movement, and that was to declare a sympathetic strike on a large scale.

'Never for a single moment, never for a solitary hour, did the men responsible for that strike toy or play with political issues. I was present at many of the meetings – not to take part in them, because I never did – but in order that I might know what was in the minds of these men, in order that I might be able, when the time came for the House of Commons to deal with the issues, to deal with them on first hand knowledge. Never for a single moment, never for an hour did I hear any man – I don't care whether he is regarded as being of the Right wing of the party or the Left wing of the party – I never heard a single member of the Trade Unions Congress General Committee whisper an idea, give a piece of advice, suggest a move or policy that was aimed at a politial issue. (Cheers.) Moreover, these men from the beginning never lost their heads as the Government did. These men from the very first day, from the very first minute after the Memorial Hall conference dispersed, had one aim in front of them, and one aim only, and that was to get an industrial situation created that would strengthen the hands of the miners to resist the encroachment the owners were making upon the standard of life of the mining population.

Government's Ultimatum.

'I have seen the Government in action. I have seen the General Council of the Trade Unions Congress in action, and, as a spectator in both cases, I tell you that if you are constitutionally-minded, if you believe in reason, if you believe in the great work you and I have put our hands to you would stand by the Trade Unions Congress methods every time. When I see my colleagues and myself pilloried as makers of strife,' Mr. MacDonald declared, 'it goes like a barbed arrow right into my soul when I remember how we have striven for peace. I am sometimes driven almost to despair regarding the future of my country. The intention is good, the masses are glorious, but your Government could not run a whelk stall. The Government closed the door on negotiations owing to an action against a newspaper which had no more to do with the matter than the man in the moon. They adopted that as a mere pretext, and when the T.U.C. sent a deputation to interview members of the Cabinet they found the doors locked and the lights turned out.

When the strike came the Government said there was a breach of contract. There was, and he (Mr. MacDonald) did not like breaches of contract, but four weeks ago in the Economy Bill the Government passed through the House of Commons the most egregious breach of contract, although it was true that the contract was only with organisations of working men. What business and what right in decency had any member of the Tory party to cast a stone at the men, even if they had been as bad as pictured in the official Government 'British Gazette'? Within a few hours of the commencement of the strike the Negotiating Committee of the T.U.C. was in continuous session and if they had not forced the hand of the Government there would have been shooting in the streets now instead of peace.

Sir Herbert Samuel offered his services to the Government before the negotiations, but they were refused. The Government of goodwill treated him like an enemy, but the General Council –

those horrible, wicked, and bloodthirsty men – went to Sir Herbert Samuel and asked for an interpretation of the Report of the Coal Commission. They worked until one and two in the morning and got an interpretation which they considered a good basis for negotiations. They considered that the strike had done what was necessary and called it off. The only body that stood for peace and negotiation and tried to avoid the inconvenience of war was the General Council, and at every point the Government thwarted them in their attempts.

Was it Successful?

'Some people ask if the general strike was a success,' Mr. MacDonald continued. 'I answer that by putting another question. Was the position of the Government after the strike the same as before? Of course it was not. If Mr. Baldwin at the end of the week before the strike had done what we asked him again and again to do there would have been no strike at all, and he did it within two days of the crying off of the strike. They had taken up an attitude two days after the strike quite different from the attitude they took up right up to the declaration of the strike. When calm-minded men get the actual documents in front of them I am calm in my conviction that their decision will be that the only people who strove with might and main for peace was the General Council of the Trade Unions Congress, and that the responsibility is on the Government which made it absolutely impossible for the General Council to do anything but what it did.'

Friday May 21 1926 p.10

VIOLENT ATTACK ON THE T.U.C.
'Most Bungled Strike in History.'

ACCUSATIONS BY MR. WHEATLEY.

In the Glasgow Labour party 'The South Side Standard,' Mr. J. Wheatley, M.P., hotly denounces the Trade Unions Congress General Council for its manner of calling off the general strike. He says:–

The workers have sustained a smashing reverse. It was not inflicted by their bosses nor due to their own weakness. It is a most astonishing result to a most magnificent effort. The struggle will surely rank as the greatest and most bungled strike in history.

To the consternation of the country the strike was called off without apparent rhyme or reason. Those of us who had left London thought, on hearing the news, that a great victory had been gained. The early reports left the impression that while the reputation of the Government had been saved, so had the position of the workers. There was to be no reduction in wages and no victimisation. Subsequent reports created doubts. Salvation was by no means complete. Still we were assured that, although for political reasons everything could not be stated publicly, a day or two would reveal that all was well. But on the following day there was a terrible revelation. Railway employees, tramway workers, and newspaper operatives were selected for victimisation. Very rapidly we were driven to the almost unbelievable conclusion that there had been an abject, unconditional surrender.

Not only had the T.U.C. deserted the miners, but they had gratuitously thrown their own members to the wolves. On the Friday we were hourly meeting noble fellows who had been dismissed and sentenced practically to starvation for themselves and their families. The bosses were snubbing and insulting the trade unions with calculated offensiveness. One wondered how on earth those trade union leaders did not even stipulate, in return for their desertion of the miners, the unconditional reinstatement of their own members. The most that Mr. Baldwin had demanded in his public speeches was a return to the position of the first of May, the day before the general strike began and the day after the miners' lock-out had taken place. The T.U.C. had given him more than he asked, and surely a great deal more than he expected.

Even now, their conduct is incomprehensible. On Friday night we had a joyous message by wireless and wire that the railway workers had been saved from the shambles. But on Saturday we had to blush again on finding that the railway unions had subscribed to very humiliating terms. In effect the railway directors had said to them, you may continue to have trade unionism on condition that you give us a written guarantee not to use it against us. And the railway unions agreed. The directors also insisted on their declaring publicly that they had been guilty of a wrongful act in striking and the unions swallowed this also.

Charge of Cowardice.

Some days must elapse before we learn accurately all the causes of the dreadful debacle. But I have no doubt that when everything is straightened out cowardice will occupy a prominent place. The qualities which distinguish men in a drawing-room, a palace, or a debating society are of little use in a vital struggle. Smart quips and polished manners play little part amidst grim realities. From the first moment of the struggle, and indeed before it, prominent Labour leaders were whining and grovelling. The day before the general strike was declared we were told by one of the men who were going out to lead us that defeat was certain. Others, of great influence, instead of going out to proclaim the justice of the workers' cause, spent their time damping the ardour of the courageous by wringing their hands and talking about the 'tragedy.' The real tragedy was that in its hour of trial the Labour movement was deserted by those in whom it had placed its greatest trust.

Now that trade unionism has been mortgaged to its enemies a new form of organisation may be necessary. But whatever may happen the workers of Britain have demonstrated that they are not the stuff of which slaves are made.

p.12

CABINET AND TRADE UNIONS.
Home Secretary on New Legislation Question.

NO HURRIED ACTION.

Addressing the special meeting of the Grand Council of the Primrose League in London yesterday, Sir William Joynson-Hicks, the Home Secretary, said that he understood Mr. Ramsay MacDonald considered that the Government was not fit to run a whelk stall.

He may be right (Sir William continued), we have never tried to, but we have rather successfully run the country during the last few days. I will not be so rude to Mr. MacDonald as to suggest that he is not fit to run a whelk stall. I think he may be quite capable of doing it. (Laughter.) But a difficulty does arise when a body of men whose capacity is that of running a whelk stall strive to run the country. (Laughter.) I would suggest that ex-Prime Ministers, who are entitled to very great respect from members of the present Government, should at least look at home before making comparisons as to the mode in which the Government are able to run any particular section of the country such as a whelk stall.

When he said that the Government had run the country he was not sure that he was correct. The country ran itself. There had been a most wonderful uprising of national spirit. Those who followed the course of events during the last few months must have realised that something of this kind had to come, that there was in the great trade union movement which had done so much for the good of the country and so much to improve the position of industrial workers, that there was underneath that movement, and working through it, a distinctly revolutionary spirit.

Russian Influence.
Mr. Ramsay MacDonald made fun of the suggestion that there was anything approaching foreign interference in the affairs of this

country. Last autumn he (Sir William) warned the trade unions that there was a distinct attempt being made by the Communist party and the National Minority Movement to get inside the trade unions and to turn them from their legitimate objects to the political and revolutionary objects of subverting the Constitution. Everything he said then had come true.

It was established beyond doubt that the trade unionists of the Third International in Moscow had been in close touch with the Left Wing of the trade union movement in Britain in order to destroy the present constitutional position. They realised perfectly well they were in a minority and that by working in the ordinary honest straightforward way through the Constitution and the ballot-box they never would be able to achieve their object of establishing a Socialist Republic in this country. They preferred to work by direct action and by quite open endeavour to seduce the army and navy from their allegience to the Crown.

The Left Wing movement got the upper hand. The old and sane trade unionists had warned trade unionists against anything in the nature of a general strike. No one was clearer than Mr. MacDonald himself as to the futility of general strikes and the harm they must do to the working people more than any other class. Surely Mr. MacDonald was now rather on the horns of a dilemma, and either the Left Wing of the trade union movement got the upper hand of the same leaders or Mr. MacDonald failed to warn his dupes of what they were running into by adopting that course. Which of these things happened the public did not know.

Success of the Volunteers.

The menace of a general strike had been a bogy for a great many years past (Sir William continued). Europe and the United States watched with the greatest intensity during the past crisis to see if Britain were made of the same stuff as one hundred years ago. To the astonishment of the world they found that the fibre of the men and women of Great Britain was as strong and steady as in the great days of the past. The Government does not take the credit. You know how well the organisation worked, and how members of the Cabinet, heads of great departments, and volunteers worked together as one team. But it was not so much that. It really was the spirit of the people. No one would have believed that a quarter of a million men would have joined the special constabulary in ten days, and they tell me that if the strike had lasted another three or four days we would have had 100,000 in London alone. That showed the marvellous determination to uphold the old Constitution, and not to allow our country to be defeated by any action of the community.

The remarkable thing was that the volunteers, and I have this officially on all hands, working with a will, did their work better and quicker than the old experts out on strike. In the docks and on the ships the number of volunteers was fewer than the old expert workers, and they did their work better and quicker. That has gone a long way to destroying the supposed necessity for the skilled workmen. If we are put to it there is no limit to what Britons can do for the sake of the country. Having once and for all said the bogy of the general strike, it will be much easier in the future. If in the future people threaten any Government with a general strike we can point to 1926 when the bubble was burst, and there was made clear the impossibility of holding up a country with the traditions and determination of Great Britain to ransom at the hands of any body or organised class.

Future of the Unions.

Dealing with the future, Sir William said: There are some of our party who are rather determined that we should take the opportunity of dealing harshly with the trade union movement. I say quite clearly that this is not the view of the Government. With a Prime Minister such as Mr. Baldwin trade unionists may be perfectly certain that no attempt will be made to destroy their legitimate position and influence in the country.

We wish them to continue their beneficent work in the interests of the industrial community, but quite definitely we do not intend that the country shall be exposed again to the risks of anything like a lightning universal strike such as that attempted recently. It is our duty to protect the country from any recurrence of that kind, but it is equally our duty not to legislate in a hurry. We have to consider very carefully and fully what can be done on one hand to protect the country, and on the other so to do it as not to injure the legitimate work of the trade unions. (Cheers.)

The last three articles are of particular significance for they are indicative of the varying interpretations that have been placed on the events of May 1926. The one viewpoint not presented is that of the mineowners. Having achieved the termination of the General Strike, the Government in the summer of 1926 attempted to persuade the Mining Association to show more flexibility in its negotiations with the MFGB. The Association, through its chief spokesman Evan Williams, however, was completely unmoved and remained firm in its determination to extract from the MFGB acceptance of district agreements and a general lowering of wage levels. The surrender of the MFGB in November and December of 1926 to the owners' terms left no doubt as to who had triumphed in the mining confrontation and salt was rubbed into the wound with the decision of the Government in 1927 to introduce legislation outlawing sympathetic strikes and reducing the ability of the unions to extract a political levy from their members.

Certain sections of the labour movement took solace in the belief that the strike had further cemented working class solidarity and had created an awareness of the ability of the labour movement to play a central role in British political life. More realistically, however, the pendulum of power in the following decade swung clearly towards those in the trade union movement and Labour Party who sought to improve their bargaining power within the existing constitutional channels rather than be associated with overtones of subversion or radical change.